Cancel THIS

Mike Fairclough

Fisher King Publishing

CANCEL THIS

Copyright © Mike Fairclough 2025

All rights reserved

Print ISBN 978-1-916776-73-9
Ebook ISBN 978-1-916776-74-6

All rights reserved. No part of this publication may be reproduced or distributed in any form or by any means, or stored in a database or electronic retrieval system, or otherwise copied for private or public use without the prior written permission of Fisher King Publishing Ltd.

No part of this book may be used or reproduced in any manner for the purpose of training artificial intelligence technologies or systems and Fisher King Publishing expressly reserves this work from the text and data mining exception.

The right of Mike Fairclough to be identified as the author of this work has been asserted by him in accordance with the Copyright, Designs and Patents act, 1988.

Published worldwide by Fisher King Publishing
fisherkingpublishing.co.uk

Cover design by Tali Digirolamo

For Sundeep Sitatra.
My brilliant, beautiful wife. A warrior queen who never bowed, never blinked, and never stayed silent.

For my children, Tali, Iggy, Luna and Star.
My fiercest freedom fighters, born with fire in their bellies and truth on their tongues.

For my granddaughter, Alice.
May your voice always be loud, your spirit unbreakable, and your future uncancelled.

For Maddy.
Alice's mum and a lioness in her own right. You've passed the torch of courage to the next generation.

This is for all of you.
Free speech warriors. Fearless souls.
Unapologetically alive.
Keep roaring.

Contents

About the Author — i

Introduction — 1

Chapter 1 - Toxic Masculinity — 7

Chapter 2 - Gender Ideology — 15

Chapter 3 - White Privilege — 21

Chapter 4 - National Pride — 27

Chapter 5 - Climate Change Alarmism — 35

Chapter 6 - Thought Crimes — 43

Chapter 7 - Trigger Warnings — 49

Chapter 8 - The War on Childhood — 59

Chapter 9 - Immigration and Border Betrayal — 67

Chapter 10 - Digital ID — 79

Chapter 11 - The Death of Satire — 85

Chapter 12 - Questioning Medical Interventions — 93

Chapter 13 - Rebellion: A British Tradition — 101

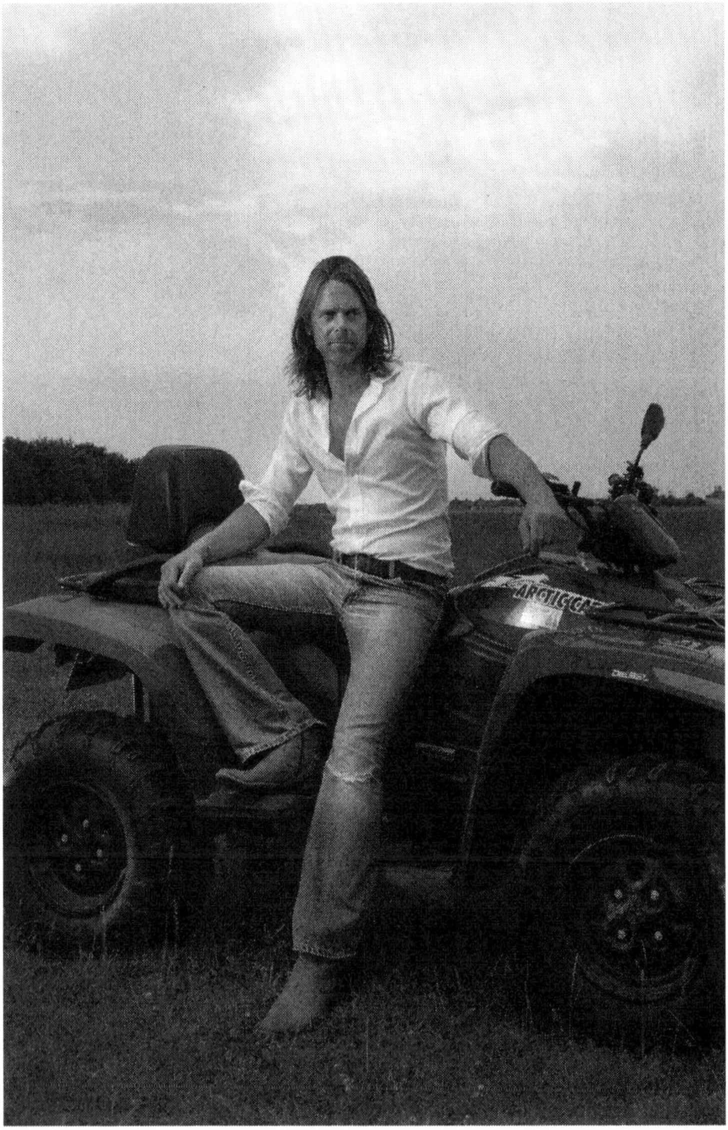

About the Author

Mike Fairclough is an internationally acclaimed educator with thirty years' experience in the field, including nineteen years as a high-profile headmaster. He has been at the forefront of character education in Britain, focusing on risk-taking, the building of resilience, and outdoor learning. He has received widespread media attention for his approach, including teaching children to fire shotguns, skin rabbits, and to cook over an open fire.

Fairclough was the only serving headteacher or school principal, out of 43,500 in the United Kingdom, to publicly question the Covid 'vaccine' rollout to children.

He is the author of five books, Playing With Fire, Wild Thing, Rewilding Childhood, Take Daily and The Hero's Voice. He is ghostwriter and editor for Kevin Anderson and Associates, a leading firm, trusted by New York Times bestselling authors, CEOs, and thought leaders, to bring their stories and ideas to life. Mike is also an editor for Fisher King Publishing, supporting outspoken authors and their works and their right to free speech.

His book, Cancel THIS, is a response to the Orwellian levels of censorship within modern Britain, and a direct challenge to cancel culture's nefarious grip on free speech.

THE PARTY TOLD YOU TO REJECT THE EVIDENCE OF YOUR EYES AND EARS. IT WAS THEIR FINAL, MOST ESSENTIAL COMMAND.

Introduction

Britain's cancel culture is a purposely designed social credit system. Say the wrong thing, and you're done for. One 'offensive' tweet? Straight to prison. Say a silent prayer? You're nicked. Point out that men don't have wombs, or that climate change hysteria is exaggerated? You're sacked and shunned. Post a meme that contradicts a government orthodoxy or expresses concerns about illegal immigration? Congrats, you're now persona non grata and at risk of being given a holiday at His Majesty's pleasure.

Welcome to the land of the free... until you express an opinion.

Great Britain, 2025, where the air is thick with sanctimonious twaddle, and our inalienable rights are under attack from the self-proclaimed elite. Those pompous, hypocritical overlords of 'correct' thinking, have decided our words, thoughts, and even our chickens need their approval. Free speech? In the U.K., members of the public are in prison for sending a single tweet. And just wait until they roll out digital ID (the so called BritCard) and the Stasi levels of censorship which will follow.

The establishment has clamped down harder than Keir Starmer on a Ukrainian rentboy. Wielding censorship like a sledgehammer and telling us what constitutes 'approved truth' as though we're living in George Orwell's *1984*.

But fear not, because there's a growing rebellion. Increasing numbers of Brits simply aren't having it anymore. They see through this dystopian farce, preferring instead to give it the middle finger. Our great nation isn't China or North Korea (though they'd like it to be). Britain is the crucible of free speech, and has long championed open expression across literature, the arts, and politics.

Amidst the madness, we salute a titan of liberty: John Milton, whose *Areopagitica* in 1644 stands as a blazing beacon for free speech. With a poet's fire and a rebel's heart, Milton faced down Parliament's suffocating book licensing laws, daring to proclaim that truth thrives only when it wrestles openly with falsehood. *"Let her and Falsehood grapple; who ever knew Truth put to the worse in a free and open encounter?"* he thundered, crafting a vision of Britain as a place for ideas, where no censor's pen could silence the quest for truth. His words, a clarion call against tyranny, sowed the seeds for our nation's proud claim as a bastion of free expression.

Let's kick off with a story so absurd it could only happen on this sceptred isle. On October 5, 2024, *The Daily Mail* ran the headline: "Defra left with egg on its face in online revolt over chicken database crashes website, as pranksters list rubber chickens and chicken nuggets as 'pets'." Our government, in a fit of bureaucratic delirium, decreed that every chicken in the land must be registered on a digital database. Why? To 'safeguard' us, naturally. The Department for Environment, Food and Rural

Affairs (DEFRA) insisted on compliance, or face the wrath of a clipboard wielding official.

Enter the Great British public, who, with a collective cry of "Not today, mate," unleashed chaos so beautiful it deserves a statue in Trafalgar Square. The website didn't just crash; it imploded. DEFRA described a, "High volume of applications," likely hundreds of thousands, as the site was flooded with fake and ludicrous entries. It was a digital uprising, a masterclass in taking the absolute piss, proving we're not a nation of drones who'll nod along to every whimsical edict. We're the land of John Locke, who told the Crown to shove its gag orders, demanding our right to speak freely without a king's boot on our throats. His fierce call for liberty in 1689 still fuels our fight against the elite's assault on freedom, from bird databases to jail time for social media posts.

This is why the establishment is 'decolonising' the English school curriculum and stamping trigger warnings on everything from Shakespeare to Aldous Huxley's *Brave New World*. In British universities, even Homer's *The Odyssey* has been flagged with warnings in classics and literature courses due to its potentially 'distressing' content. The ruling class don't want us to be inspired by stories of heroism, resistance, battling against the odds, and vanquishing evil. They prefer us to be fearful and obedient.

This, my friends, is the beating heart of *Cancel THIS*. Sometimes, you've just got to refuse to play the game. Mocking the authorities and saying, "No! I'm not doing it!" It's signing up your nan's ceramic cockerel to a government database just to watch the system choke. It's laughing at the po-faced establishment who lecture us on what to think and say. These hypocrites, with their private jets and public scoldings, want to police your speech, social media posts, and your thoughts. They'll cancel you faster than a reality show reject if you dare step out of line. And for what? To protect their grip on the 'truth.'

Silence and doing nothing are no longer viable options. Not if we want our children and grandchildren to inherit the country our forebears sacrificed their lives for. Every time you bite your tongue or self-censor to avoid the mob, you're handing them the keys to your mind. Our silence is their power. Compliance is the last thing we should agree to. If you let them, they'll have you bowing to their every whim and agreeing to unimaginable horrors.

That's why *Cancel THIS* is part survival guide, part rebellious handbook, and a salute to the dissidents, oddballs, and anyone who's ever been told to shut up and behave. We don't just resist; we do it with flair, with bollocks, and with our signature British humour. We're the nation of the stiff upper lip, the victors of two world wars, and we laid the foundation for free speech with the Magna Carta in 1215. We have a long history of curbing tyrants and fighting for freedom.

This book also shines a light on the agenda behind the bullshit. It's no accident that almost every government in the world has turned on its citizens at the same time. Pushing harmful and illogical ideologies, punishing dissidents, and seeding fear about everything from the weather through to the common cold. It's all part of a vision which is laid out by the likes of the United Nations and which our government has signed up to. So, buckle up, tell the woke police to sod off, and let's rip into this global circus of pompous 'elites' who think they can nanny us into submission.

This book is your guide to living freely in a world gone mad. It's about laughing in the face of censorship, ignoring the establishment's nonsensical rules, and embracing the global fight for free speech with true grit and resilience.

Let's keep the rebellion rolling, one glorious piss take at a time.

DIGITAL ID
YOU'LL OWN NOTHING
AND SCAN
EVERYTHING

Chapter 1 - Toxic Masculinity

Never Mind the Bollocks: In Defence of Real Men, Real Grit, and a Nation With Balls.

Let's just get this out of the way: masculinity isn't toxic. What's toxic is pretending it is. What's toxic is demonising testosterone like it's anthrax and acting like strong men are some sort of threat to civilisation. The truth is, strong men built civilization, and when it comes crashing down, it's going to be the men with calloused hands and spines of steel who put the pieces back together. Empowered women will rebuild it too. But as equals who can handle strong men.

And here's the truth: women love real men. Not the neutered, beige, emotionally apologetic caricatures pushed by lifestyle bloggers with seventeen cats and zero sex appeal. We're talking about men who take up space. Who stand for something. Who make their kids feel safe just by walking into the room.

This isn't nostalgia. It's rebellion.

To be absolutely clear, I'm not talking about men who beat and abuse women, or men who pretend to be women and abuse real women in sports. Nor do I include within the ranks of real men those who harm children. All of the above are misogynists, mentally ill, and anything but masculine.

CANCEL THIS

True masculinity was forged in the fire of our ancestors and is as ancient as the hills. That's why it's under attack.

Let's talk bollocks for a minute. Literal ones. Because here's the quiet war no one wants to admit: they're coming for your nuts.

No, seriously.

They've been slashing testosterone levels for decades. Through plastic in your water, soy in your food, and fear in your soul. They want a man who won't fight back. A man who won't question authority. A man who'll sit down, shut up, and apologise for things he didn't do.

Why?

Because masculine men are hard to control.

A man with a backbone won't swallow the nonsense. He won't bow to the mob or change his opinion because Karen on LinkedIn got offended. He won't accept being told he's 'problematic' for having boundaries and opinions.

This isn't conspiracy, it's common sense. If you want to control a population, you don't start with their politics. You start with their identity. You start by telling them they're bad just for being who they are.

But here's the truth they can't cancel: it's entirely possible that everything that's happened: every war, every failure, every revolution, has led us precisely to this point. The reckoning. The golden mean. The da Vinci code of awakening. We're on the brink of a cultural Fibonacci spiral, where everything that was lost returns in sacred sequence. And at the centre of that spiral?

Manhood. Not the Instagram-filtered version. The real thing.

The kind of masculinity that carried stretchers at the Somme. That stood against fascism with nothing but resolve and a Lee-Enfield rifle. The kind that walked miles through the Blitz rubble to get to a factory job, then raised a family on four quid and a slap.

My grandfathers fought in two world wars. My paternal grandfather fought in World War 1 at the Battle of the Somme. My maternal grandfather was a prisoner in World War 2 and survived the thousand mile walk to freedom from his incarceration at the hands of the Nazis. They didn't ask for safe spaces or cry about microaggressions. They had PTSD before it had a name. Yet they still showed up. They were flawed. They were human. And they were strong. That's masculinity. That's heritage.

And no, this isn't about men versus women. That's another trap. Strong men don't hate women. They protect them. They honour them. They attract them. Because real masculinity doesn't shrink others to feel tall. It lifts everyone with it.

The fight for free speech is not just a male thing. Women like J.K. Rowling have risked careers, reputations, and livelihoods to speak the truth in a culture that tells you to shut up or be burned at the digital stake. She's taken more fire than most. Armed with nothing but her pen and her spine. That's British grit. That's courage. And that is what rebellion looks like.

This is about energy. Polarity. Purpose. The sacred dance of opposites that keeps nature in balance. When you demonise one side, it weakens the whole.

Britain has always been the awkward dinner guest at the empire table. From Boudica to the Sex Pistols, from the Magna Carta to Orwell, from Churchill's defiance to pub landlords telling the smoking ban to piss off after six pints, we are a nation of glorious, incorrigible rebels.

And let's not forget our famous British free speech heritage. We invented the art of saying outrageous things with a straight face. We pioneered satire. We turned political incorrectness into an Olympic sport. You think banning opinions will stop us? Mate, we survived the Luftwaffe, and we beat them into the ground.

It is time to reclaim it all. To stand tall, speak loudly, and rattle the establishment's cage. Not with rage, but with certainty. With intention. With charm. With the kind of masculine confidence that is empowered and in service of family and our communities.

So, if you're tired of being told to pipe down, tired of feeling ashamed for simply being a man, stand up and speak out.

Ultimately, the authorities and the woke mob are anything but empowered. They're scared. They can see the growing ranks of real men and see that our power is rising. We rise along with our sacred and empowered women. This is what terrifies the tyrants.

So, never mind the bollocks. Real men are back.

Top Rebellion Tips

1. Grow a Beard So Majestic, It Gets Misgendered as a Hate Crime

Nothing rattles the soy-scented gender studies brigade like a proper beard. Not a sculpted hipster one. A full, unapologetic, Viking forest. One that says, "I've chopped wood, fixed a leaking roof, and defended freedom before breakfast." Let them stare. Let HR file a complaint. You're not here to be pretty. You're here to *exist loudly* with testicles and timber.

2. Start a Men's Group - A Proper One

Meet weekly. No safe spaces. No lattes. Just strong tea, stronger opinions, and the kind of conversations that would give a Guardian columnist a hernia. Agenda? Fix bikes. Raise sons. Mock nonsense. Plan how to take Britain back from the Ministry of Feelings. Dress code: flannel, grit, and a spine.

3. Redefine 'Toxic Masculinity' as 'You'll Be Grateful For When the Heating Breaks'

Because the same people who whinge about 'masculine energy'

are the first to call Dave the plumber when their boiler dies at 2am. Real masculinity isn't toxic. It's what fixes your electrics, defends your freedoms, and hauls you out of floodwater without updating their Instagram first. Call it toxic all you like. Just don't call it *after hours*.

4. Make Chivalry Great Again

Hold doors. Stand up when a lady enters. Carry the heavy stuff. Not because women are weak, but because you are *strong* and you bloody well should. Watch as half the room melts in appreciation and the other half self-combusts from ideological indigestion. Either way, you win.

6. Ladies, If He'd Rather 'Raise Awareness' Than Raise His Voice, He's Not a Man, He's a Mascot.

When the mob comes for your job, your kids, or your right to speak, you don't need a man who posts hashtags. You need one who stands up, squares his shoulders, and says, "Over my dead body."

Because if he's not ready to fight for you, he's just another accessory in your handbag.

So, here's to the men with grit in their guts, fire in their bellies, and bollocks where bollocks are meant to be. The ones who don't need a safe space because they *are* the safe space. Who protect what matters, stand for what's right, and still know how to change a tyre, throw a punch, and make a woman laugh without apologising for existing.

The age of beige is over.

Masculinity isn't dying. It's just been doing push-ups in the shed, waiting for its cue.

SOVEREIGNTY IS
AN OBSTACLE TO
GLGBAL GOVERNANCE..
MIGRATION IS ONE OF
THE ENGINES TO
RESHAPE SOCIETY.
GEORGE SOROS

Chapter 2 - Gender Ideology

Chicks with Dicks: Gender Ideology and the Great British Piss-Take

Welcome to Clown Island, population: us! The gender ideology circus has pitched its psychedelic tent smack in the middle of dear old Blighty, and the ringleaders are flogging more crap than a car boot sale in Croydon.

This isn't just a culture war. It's a full-blown assault on reality. Call a bloke a bloke and suddenly you're public enemy number one. Biology? That's now considered hate speech. The rainbow commissars don't just want your compliance, they want your soul, served with a side of pronouns and rainbow lanyards.

But there's also good news: Britain's not dead yet. Beneath the layers of wokery, under the weight of government approved thoughtcrime, the Great British piss-take is alive and kicking. It's time we reminded the world that we didn't survive this long just to be told that 'men can lactate.'

In defence of truth, sanity, and good old-fashioned common sense, buckle up buttercup. Let's dive into the madness.

It's a Cult

Let's not be coy: gender ideology is the intellectual equivalent of licking batteries. It's the deranged belief that you can switch sex like you're changing train platforms at King's Cross. A lad with stubble and a set of plums says he's a bird, and the state expects you to nod like a Churchill dog on speed. Say 'hang on a minute' and you're labelled a far right fascist faster than you can say, 'XX chromosomes.'

We're living in a parody written by Aldous Huxley, directed by Monty Python, and funded by the taxpayer. Every institution, from your local council to the Church of England, has bent the knee to this nonsense. They've swapped truth for 'lived experience,' and objectivity for feelings. It's not inclusivity; it's ideological indoctrination with rainbow flags.

And God help you if you object. One tweet, one meme, one question, and suddenly you're being dragged before HR like you're a witch in the Inquisition. Only instead of fire and brimstone, it's Zoom calls and 'unconscious bias training.'

Ancient Balls

Cast your mind back to the ancients, those toga-wearing legends who knew a thing or two about reality. Theseus didn't mince his words, he defeated monsters. The gender ideology mob? They're today's Minotaur: half nonsense, half narcissism, demanding sacrifices on the altar of 'affirmation.'

Think of Hercules, facing the Hydra of progressive lunacy. You chop off 'preferred pronouns,' and up pops 'genderfluid unicorn pronouns' and 'ze/zir bathrooms.' He didn't host a seminar. He burned the bastard to ash. Our fire? Mockery. Good, honest, merciless British mockery. Think Sid James meets Ricky Gervais with a pint in hand. When they say 'chest-feeding,' you say 'sod off.'

Achilles? His only weak spot was his heel. Ours? Apparently, our ability to think critically. But we're also the country that invented sarcasm as a national sport. We built Britain with brass balls, dry wit, and the ability to keep a straight face while telling someone they're talking utter bollocks.

So how do we fight back against ideological tyranny?

Top Rebellion Tips

1. Talk Back

Speak truth like it's 1940 and the doodle bugs are overhead. Refuse to play the pronoun charade. They want silence. Give them a speech.

2. Take the Absolute Piss

Laughter kills tyranny. From Chaucer to Clarkson, we've weaponised wit. Memes, banter, innuendo, use them all. Take their sacred cows and stick a traffic cone on them. Mock 'birthing people' until the term curls up and dies of shame.

3. Pronouns? Just Use 'Mate' and Watch the Room Detonate

Forget the minefield of 'ze/zir/unicorn-self.' Just call everyone *mate*. It's gender-neutral, offensively British, and guaranteed to enrage the sort of person who thinks their pronouns belong in your email signature. Try it in HR: "Alright mate, just here for my thought-crime review." Boom. Detonation complete.

4. Host a Woke Exorcism at Your Local School Fayre

Set up a stall between the tombola and the cake raffle. For £1 a go, you can rid little Timmy of gender unicorns, DEI goblins, and the demon of 'preferred pronouns.' Free stickers for every child who correctly identifies a boy as a boy. Bonus points if you serve tea out of a 'Men Can't Get Periods' mug.

5. Hold the Bloody Line

Don't flinch. Don't apologise. Don't bend the knee. This ideology is a house of cards. Say "No," loudly and often, and watch the thing wobble. It only survives because ordinary people are too cowardly to call it bollocks.

6. The Last Stand before we become Clown Island

This is our Thermopylae. Our Dunkirk. Our final stand at the gates of sanity. They've got NGO's, HR departments and the civil service. We've got sarcasm, common sense, and the moral clarity of a pissed-off Yorkshireman. That'll do nicely.

So, here's to the rebels, to Rowling, to the sacked teachers, to the ordinary Brits who still believe that reality matters more than feelings. Let's make this island a stronghold of sense in a sea of madness.

Truth will out. Keep the banter brutal. And for God's sake, keep calling a spade a spade. And a man a man.

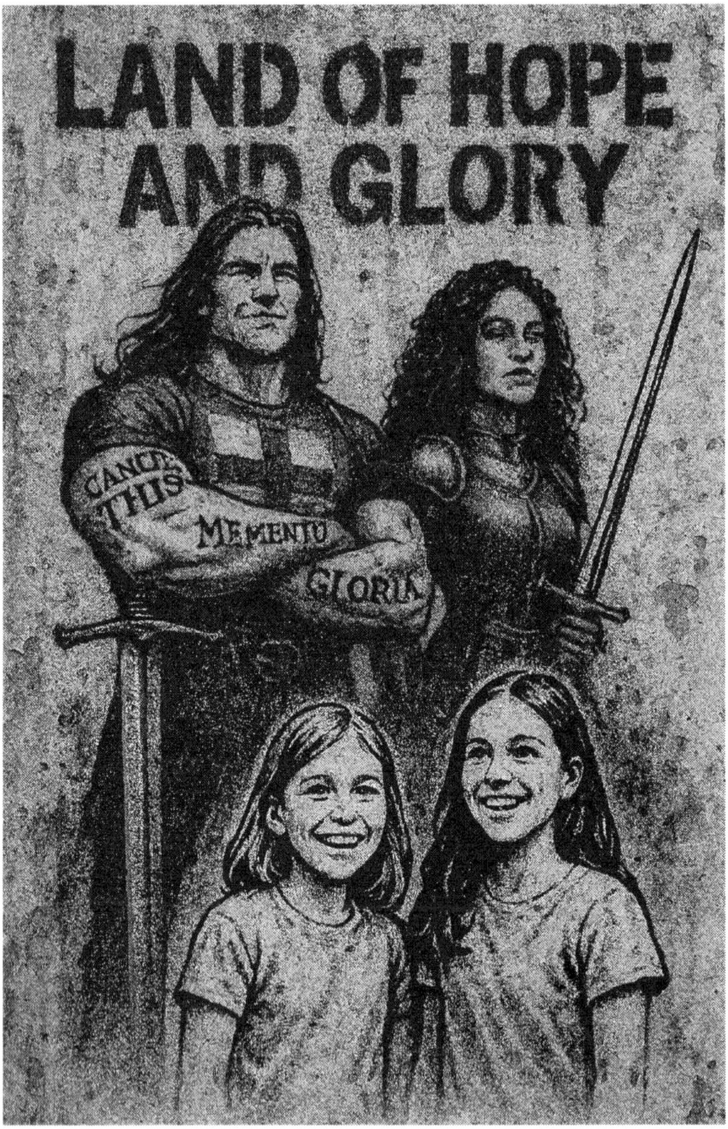
LAND OF HOPE
AND GLORY
THIS

Chapter 3 - White Privilege

White Privilege and Other Middle Class Fairy Tales

Let me get one thing out of the way before some Guardian-reading Twitter activist anonymously reports me (again!): I'm married to a dark-skinned Punjabi Indian woman. A brilliant, strong, brown woman. I love her. We have curry nights *and* arguments about DIY. I've never been to an EDL rally. I don't own a copy of *Mein Kampf*. And I believe racism, against anyone, is abhorrent.

That said, let's have a proper chat about this thing we're all apparently swimming in like goldfish: white privilege.

Because I keep hearing that phrase thrown about like it's some sort of universal truth. It's taught in schools, mumbled in HR meetings, and uttered like a religious mantra on the BBC. *White privilege*, we're told, is everywhere. It's like oxygen.

But it doesn't actually add up. Not historically. Not factually. Not even in terms of basic common sense.

Here's the funny bit (and by funny, I mean depressing): if you challenge the idea of white privilege, even politely, people act like you've just invaded Poland.

A Brief History of White Squalor

Let's rewind. Britain during the colonial age. The time we're all told white people were skipping around with parasols, drinking tea, and plundering the globe like posh pirates. It was a hellhole for most white people. Have you ever seen pictures of Victorian children working down mines? 8 years old, half-starved, and covered in coal dust.

Only a tiny 'elite' of whites: aristocrats, royals, slavers, and empire-backed businessmen, profited from colonialism. The average Brit? Mucking coal, dying young, and living ten to a room. Empire made a few men rich and left the rest coughing in chimneys. It's always been about class, not colour.

Fast Forward: White, Male, and Homeless

Fast forward to today, and apparently not much has changed, except the slums have Wi-Fi and Deliveroo. Because if white privilege is real, someone forgot to send the memo to:

- The white war veteran sleeping rough in a London underpass,
- The kid from a sink estate who just got stabbed for his phone.
- And the working-class white lads now bottom of the table in educational achievement.

But you won't hear much about that on BBC Radio 4. It doesn't fit the narrative. It means the middle-class academics pushing the 'white privilege' narrative might have to admit they're more privileged than the bloke who fixes their boiler. So instead, they pretend that race trumps everything.

It's not racist to say that grouping all white people together as 'privileged' is, well… a bit racist.

Imagine telling a single mum on benefits in Blackpool she's had it easy because her ancestors *might* have lived near someone who *once* owned a plantation. Go on, tell her. I'll wait.

Where Do We Go From Here?

Now, none of this is to say racism doesn't exist. It does. I've seen it, I've called it out. And I'll keep doing it, whether it's aimed at black people, brown people, or pasty white lads. But if your entire worldview is built on the idea that skin colour = power, then you've missed the entire bloody point of Britain's history, and its present.

Because being white doesn't make you privileged. Being rich, powerful, or born into the right postcode might. But skin tone? That's just packaging. It doesn't mean there isn't gold inside.

Maybe take a stroll down any British high street and have a look around. Not everyone in a Weatherspoons or sleeping rough is part of an oppressive ruling elite.

Funny how white privilege always skips the bloke freezing in a doorway with three blankets. Apparently privilege now comes with food banks, eviction notices, and a sleeping bag on the high street.

Call out racism wherever you see it. And hold the people who are shafting everyone, of every colour, to account. The self-proclaimed elite (of every race) who want us divided and fighting amongst ourselves. The real divide was never black and white. It's always been top and bottom.

For those who don't want to embrace being white: A Beginner's Guide for the Terminally Ashamed

Step 1: Master the Art of Apologising for Everything Your Great-Great-Great-Grandad May or May Not Have Done

Before you even think about enjoying a cuppa or putting milk in first like a savage, you must apologise. Constantly. Apologise for the Empire, the Crusades, and that time a white man invented the lightbulb, which is now apparently a symbol of colonialism. Be prepared to apologise for your skin tone every time you enter a university campus, a vegan café, or a BBC panel show. Bonus points if you can weep softly into a soy latte while doing it.

Step 2: Accessorise Like a Woke Anthropologist

If you're white and want to survive modern Britain, remember: cultural appropriation is a crime unless you're middle-class and doing it ironically. So, ditch your flat cap and embrace *ethically sourced* incense, Indonesian tattoos, and a 'Namaste' doormat. You may not have heat in winter, but your living room will smell fantastic. Just don't, under any circumstances, enjoy your own culture. Morris dancing is colonial violence and roast dinners are oppressive.

Step 3: Pretend You're Oppressing Someone, Even When You're Being Mugged

You might be a white lad from Hull living on beans and knock-off Monster, but don't forget: you're the problem. If someone robs you, it's probably your fault (systemic power dynamics and all that). If you question this, remind yourself that the sociology graduate behind the Guardian op-ed knows more about your life than you do. You're not working-class You're *structurally violent*. Now go and apologise to your smart meter.

But you know what makes Britain great? We take the piss. Out of everything. Even ourselves. Especially ourselves. We laugh through disaster, make jokes at funerals, and carry on. With humour, sarcasm, and a strong cup of tea. And that's the real privilege: being able to laugh, no matter how bleak it gets. So, sod the guilt, bin the shame, and don't let some blue-haired Twitter warrior tell you you're the bad guy because your great-great-granddad owned a spade.

And if some quinoa-munching diversity officer with a gender studies degree wants to call you 'problematic' for existing, smile, wave, and remind them their entire worldview collapses the moment the Wi-Fi goes down.

You don't need to kneel, apologise, or identify as a tree to be a good person. Just tell the truth, crack a joke, and pass the bloody biscuits. Because in the end, we're not here to be liked. We're here to live, laugh, and enjoy being who we are. The concept of white privilege is a scam.

Chapter 4 - National Pride

When Saying, "I Quite Like Britain," is Treated Like a Confession at the Hague

Love Britain and eating sausage rolls? Steady on, Mosley!

Remember when waving a Union Jack just meant you liked your country and *maybe* had a Greggs sausage roll in one hand and a warm pint in the other? Simple times. These days? Waving the national flag is seen as a far-right dog whistle, probably followed by a police visit and a stern chat about 'inclusive values' while someone wearing three lanyards hands you a pamphlet on decolonising your tea bags.

Honestly, we've reached the point where *liking* your own country is controversial. You can identify as a woodland mushroom and get a round of applause on BBC Breakfast. But say, "I think Britain's alright actually," and suddenly you're one goose-step away from being banned from Sainsbury's.

God forbid you mention Churchill. The bloke literally helped defeat the Nazis. *THE Nazis*. But apparently, that's not good enough anymore. Nope. Some avocado-chomping third-year sociology student with a fringe like a sheepdog has decided that

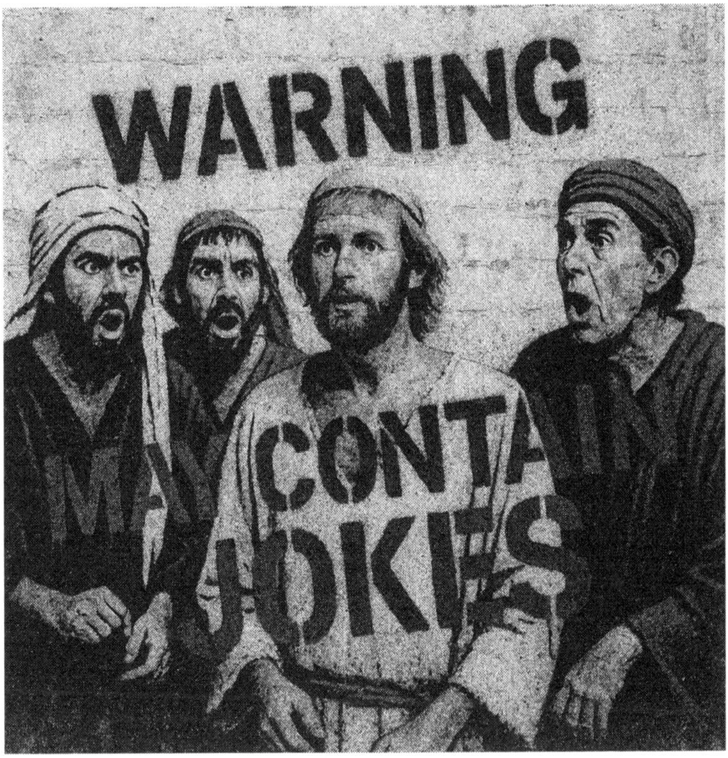
WARNING

Winston was a bit *problematic*, and now every statue of him needs a trigger warning and a safe space.

It's mental

These people walk past gang stabbings in broad daylight, ignore actual modern slavery in Leicester sweatshops, and then get *fuming* because someone said the Empire wasn't 100% evil. "You can't celebrate Empire Day!" Right. But you can celebrate *Gender-Neutral Vegan Month* and we all have to clap like trained seals or risk being called 'literally Hitler.'

You couldn't make it up

People talk about Britain like it's a malignant tumour. You've got MPs saying the flag makes them 'uncomfortable.' Sorry, what? You're a *Member of Parliament* in *Britain*. If the sight of your own flag makes you feel ill, maybe try *not working for the country it represents*. Imagine turning up to work at McDonald's and bursting into tears at the sight of a cheeseburger. You'd be sectioned.

Let's be honest, some of these people don't want to decolonise history, they want to *delete* it. Tear down statues, rename streets, bin Shakespeare because apparently *Julius Caesar* isn't intersectional enough. What next? Blur out the Stonehenge because it's 'problematic to druids?'

And now the political establishment has voted to abort perfectly healthy babies (using any means) right up to the day of birth, and to 'assist the suicide' of burdensome sick people. Would they extend this to people who are disabled (as they do in Canada). Of course they will.

If you love Britain and have any allegiance for the old and the young who live here, it's time to stand up and speak out.

Every time someone tries to say, "Hang on, maybe Britain did a couple of decent things, like antibiotics and the Mini Cooper," they're instantly accused of pining for the Raj and secretly polishing a monocle.

Here's the thing, no country's perfect. Not one. But the British invented common law, free speech, football, and queueing, for Christ's sake. That's civilisation, right there. We've apologised for half our past already, more times than Piers Morgan's been sacked, and yet it's *never enough*. There are people who want us to apologise for things we didn't even do.

And while we're at it, what is it with this obsession over statues? "This one's offensive." "That one's oppressive." Mate, it's a statue. It's a big lump of rock. It's not shouting slurs. It's not enslaving your nan. If you're losing sleep over what a lump of bronze did 200 years ago, you need less activism and more fibre.

Meanwhile, the actual country is falling apart. Roads full of potholes. NHS collapsing like a soufflé in a sauna. And what are they focused on? Whether Captain Cook's memorial is 'problematic to indigenous feelings.' He's dead. You're on an iPhone. Move on.

We've gone from *Rule, Britannia!* to *Apologise, Britannia!* And it's not even guilt anymore. It's fashion. Trendy shame.

Newsflash: patriotism isn't fascism. Being proud of your country doesn't mean you want to start goose-stepping down the high street in Union Jack underpants. It just means you like living here. You like beans on toast and making jokes about the weather.

And yet we're raising a generation that thinks pride is toxic and pessimism is virtue. Don't celebrate anything. Everything's colonial, everything's offensive.

If you're going to live here, eat the food, enjoy the freedoms, use the Wi-Fi, and then slag it off 24/7, at least do it with a bit of perspective. Because if you tried this performative national self-loathing in China or Saudi Arabia, you'd disappear faster than a BBC comedy show that jokes about gender fluidity.

So, here's to Britain: land of queuing, sarcasm, dodgy weather, and glorious contradiction. A place where you're free to say, "Britain's crap," but you can't wave your own flag at a national event without being compared to Mussolini. Maybe, just maybe, we've lost the plot.

Top Rebellion Tips

1. Start a 'Problematic Pride' Parade

Since expressing national pride is now considered a microaggression in some university common rooms, somewhere between cultural appropriation and saying, "Good morning," without checking someone's pronouns, it's time to go all in.

Organise a full-blown Problematic Pride Parade. Picture it: Union Jack bunting fluttering like Orwellian rebellion, sausage rolls skewered like tiny pork-based Excaliburs, and *The Rolling Stones* blasting from a Morris Minor draped in bunting last seen during the Queen's Silver Jubilee.

Invite an army of pensioners with poppies, bricklayers who quote Kipling between pints, and that one English teacher who still insists on reading Tennyson aloud 'because the meter demands it.' Include a Latin chant of the *Magna Carta*, not because anyone understands it, but because it sounds like you're summoning liberty from a time before Wi-Fi.

2. Subvert the System: Patriotic Microaggressions

Fight back quietly by committing *patriotic microaggressions* in everyday life. Casually hum 'Land of Hope and Glory' in HR meetings. Wear socks with the Union Jack to your next 'decolonising the curriculum' seminar. Gently correct someone who calls Shakespeare a bigot by quoting him... in iambic pentameter. When someone says. "Britain's never done anything good," smile warmly, offer them a custard cream, and whisper, "Except inventing the language you're using to insult it."

Then slowly sip your tea like a Bond villain and let the awkward silence do the rest.

3. Play the Victim: Oppressed Briton Syndrome (OBS)

Two can play the oppression game. Declare yourself a sufferer of *OBS – Oppressed Briton Syndrome*. Symptoms include involuntary tea consumption, strong feelings for red phone boxes, and emotional distress at the sight of defaced Churchill statues. Demand a safe space with Union Jack beanbags and call for the decolonisation of ironic beard oil. If anyone challenges you, accuse them of being 'nationalityist' and report them to PREVENT.

4. Create a Trigger Warning for Everything British

Go full parody. Stick 'TRIGGER WARNING: CONTAINS BRITISH VALUES' signs on things like cheddar cheese, umbrellas, and the phrase 'cheers, mate.' Print fake health warnings on pork pies: *'May contain traces of empire.'* Insist that weather forecasts come with disclaimers about colonial rainfall. The goal? To turn the entire country into a satire so precise, even the wokest activist can't tell whether you're mocking them or inviting them to a reenactment of the Battle of Hastings

This island may be battered, but it's not broken. We are not a nation of cowards, censors, or culture-less drones. We are a nation of rebels, poets, inventors, piss-takers, and lionhearts. We survived the Luftwaffe. We'll survive this national identity crisis too.

Being proud to be British isn't about pretending everything's perfect. It's about loving your home while still taking the piss out of it. That's the magic. That's our edge. We don't need permission to be proud. We just need reminding that we still can be.

They can take down statues. They can rewrite textbooks. They can call us every name under the sun. But they can't cancel pride. Not real pride. The quiet, unshakeable kind that lives in every ordinary Brit who still gives a damn.

This is your country. Own it. Love it. Defend it. With words, with wit, with the full force of your British spine.

And if they don't like it? Tell them to jog on. Preferably in French. With subtitles. And a full English in your hand.

Chapter 5 - Climate Change Alarmism

Blocking the Sun, Buggering the Congo - The Climate Con

Climate alarmism is everywhere. Fortunately, the Great British Bollocks Radar is onto it.

The climate is in crisis. We know this because the people who fly private jets to climate conferences keep telling us. With tears in their eyes and designer hemp shirts on their backs, they look down at us from their solar-powered yachts and beg us to 'do our bit.' Apparently, 'our bit' involves giving up meat, driving wind-up cars, and being grateful that we're still freezing our nuts off in Britain.

England. A country where it's somehow both too hot and too cold, sometimes in the same afternoon, and where daring to ask *any* questions about climate policy now puts you in a social gulag. Speak up and you'll be exiled to the same corner of society as anyone who still uses the word 'bloke.'

They say 'trust the science.' Which science? The one that changes every three years and bans dissent? We've moved from 'global warming' to 'climate change' to 'climate emergency' to 'There's too many humans on the planet. We need to kill you.' They'll soon be charging us per exhalation.

THE ODYSSEY HOMER
SHAKESPEARE
ROALD DAHL
CHAUCER
1984
BRAVE NEW WORLD
HUXLEY

We're told CO_2 is the root of all evil. Forget war, famine, genocide. No, the real enemy is the invisible molecule that makes your veg grow. China? Oh, just 30% of global emissions, not to worry. But Britain's 1%, *that's* the problem. Quick, turn off your boiler or we're all going to drown.

Meanwhile, the world's militaries, who do love a bit of carbon, chuck out more emissions than most countries. The U.S. military alone emits more than Denmark. But don't worry, that doesn't count. Apparently bombs are eco-friendly now. War is sustainable. Just ask NATO.

And then there's the Congo. Ah yes, the ethical heart of green energy. Tens of thousands of children digging cobalt with their bare hands so that influencers in Notting Hill can post filtered Instagram pics of their new Tesla while quoting David Attenborough. But don't you dare mention this. If you even suggest that modern slavery isn't all that progressive, you're branded a fossil fuel shill and escorted out of the conversation by an angry vegan.

This is what we're calling 'progress.'

Today's green movement isn't about saving the planet. It's about optics. It's about power. It's about making sure we can't drive our car without feeling like we're clubbing a seal. Meanwhile, the real pollution: mining, military, mega-corporations, is swept under the eco-friendly rug, which is, ironically, made of recycled plastic and microfibres that end up in the sea.

And let's not forget the 'latest' bright idea from the British government: 'solar geoengineering.' Translation? Blocking out the bloody sun. No, really. £57 million has been funnelled into *dimming sunlight* to cool the earth. So, we're now actively trying to make Britain even colder than it already is. What could go wrong?

This is the same government, by the way, which wants *mandatory* solar panels on every new home by 2027. Yes, the same sunlight they're trying to block. Make it make sense.

Also, and I swear this isn't satire: they're now worried that Russia might weaponize weather control to ruin our crops. The same people who have announced that they are dimming the sun have said that dimming the sun is an act of war (which, by the way, it is).

But don't laugh. Laughing is problematic now. Apparently, mocking billionaires for flying private to climate conferences is 'undermining the message.' Well, maybe the message needs undermining if it only works when delivered by hypocrites standing on tarmac.

Instead of focusing on things which actually help the environment and humanity: like planting trees, cleaning rivers, or literally not enslaving children, they're obsessed with 'net zero,' 'carbon passports,' and turning every city into a 15-minute Orwellian wet dream. You'll own nothing, go nowhere, and be told it's *liberating*.

They promise a green utopia, but it smells suspiciously like a control grid wrapped in a spinach wrap. Today's climate crusade is a modern Hydra: chop off 'net zero,' and up pops 'carbon passports.'

We get smart meters that spy on us, apps that restrict our travel, and policies drafted by people who clearly don't practice what they preach. This is why wit, rebellion, the glorious British urge to take the piss are needed now. Because nothing deflates pomposity like satire. And these people are *aching* to be mocked.

Bill Gates talks about offsetting his carbon footprint while flying in a jet heavier than the truth. "I plant trees," he says. So do squirrels, Bill. You don't see them doing TED Talks.

You don't need a PhD to spot hypocrisy. Just eyes. And perhaps a sarcasm gland that hasn't been numbed by the BBC.

So, plant a tree, not because the UN said so, but because it's yours. Roast your steak rare. Drive your car. Say what you bloody think. They can block the sun, but they can't block your voice.

Not yet anyway.

Speak truth like you're dodging bombs in the Blitz. Nothing kills dogma like a laugh. Meme Gates' jets into oblivion. Turn their pious buzzwords into pub gags.

Top Rebellion Tips

1. 'Trust the Science' - Unless It's Tuesday, Then It's Changed Again

They told us it was global warming. Then it was climate change. Then it was a 'climate emergency.' Now it's 'we must block out the sun.' Science, apparently, now works like iTunes updates.

Start asking awkward questions. Loudly, and in public. Write 'TRUST THE SCIENCE (WHICH ONE?)' on a T-shirt and wear it to a council meeting. Mock their contradictions with memes, pub jokes, and open mic nights. Ridicule is a British birthright. Wield it like a sarcastic lightsaber.

2. The Green Revolution: Powered by Child Labour and Middle-Class Guilt

While the BBC sobs over polar bears, kids in the Congo are digging for your mate's hybrid car battery. But don't worry, Sandra from Surrey just switched to oat milk, so the planet's probably fine.

Boycott virtue-signalling tech. Drive an old petrol banger with pride and slap a bumper sticker on it that says, *'Child Labour-Free Since '03.'* Call out fake ethics. If someone lectures you about carbon footprints while holding an iPhone, ask them how their lithium's doing. If it makes them uncomfortable, you're doing God's work.

3. Welcome to Britain 2050: No Cars, No Meat, No Sun. But At Least We've Got Wind Turbines

You're trapped in your 15-minute city, cooking lentils under a grey dystopian sky, while your smart meter tells you you've used too much toast energy. But hey, at least we're saving the world for Bezos' rocket ship.

Eat the steak. Drive the car. Roast vegans at dinner parties (verbally, of course). Start an underground *Meat & Motor Club* (like Fight Club, but with bacon and petrol). Say no to digital IDs, laugh in the face of carbon passports, and whenever someone says 'net zero,' ask if that includes their private jet emissions.

4. Back the Obvious: Real Environmentalism, Not the Corporate Cosplay

Plant trees. Clean rivers. Protect wildlife. Not because Klaus Schwab said so, but because you *actually* care. Nature doesn't need more acronyms; it needs less nonsense.

Sod 'carbon credits' traded like Pokémon cards for hedge funds. If you wouldn't trust the government to run a pub quiz, don't let them redesign the weather.

Don't flinch when they call you a 'climate denier' that's just woke for 'asked a question.' Instead, point out the child labour, the eco-exempt military budgets, the virtue-signalling billionaire class jetting around like Bond villains.

So, here's to the troublemakers, the sacked scientists, the shushed sceptics, the Brits who smell a rat when Keir Starmer meets with Bill Gates and Black Rock CEO, Larry Fink. Let's make this land a fortress of reason, where questions aren't treason and hypocrisy gets a proper pasting. Keep the wit wicked, the debate wide open.

Climate alarmism is one of the greatest battle grounds for common sense. And you're on the frontline.

Chapter 6 - Thought Crimes

Thought Crime & Divine Misdemeanours: When Praying Gets You Nicked

Hush now, heretic! In Great Britain, members of the public have been arrested for the heinous crime of *thinking* too loudly near abortion clinics. Yep, silent prayer. literally standing there, saying nothing, but pondering the Almighty. Why? Because of Public Spaces Protection Orders (PSPOs) and buffer zone rules, which are basically 'no thinking allowed' zones around clinics. It's now illegal to have a quiet word with God in your head.

The coppers and councils claim that this is about stopping 'intimidation,' but in reality it's the ushering in of the 'thought police!' It's sparked fierce debate about whether you're allowed to think and pray freely without being carted off to the nick.

Britain's cancel culture is a digital Tower of Babel, a creaking arena of control, chaos, and crucifixion for anyone bold enough to whisper truth. It's a social credit system designed to turn the faithful into cowards. Say the wrong thing? You're excommunicated. Quote a bit of Corinthians? Bigot alert! Speak from the heart with honest intent? Burn the heretic!

Welcome to the new inquisition, where the stakes are your job, your reputation, and your peace of mind.

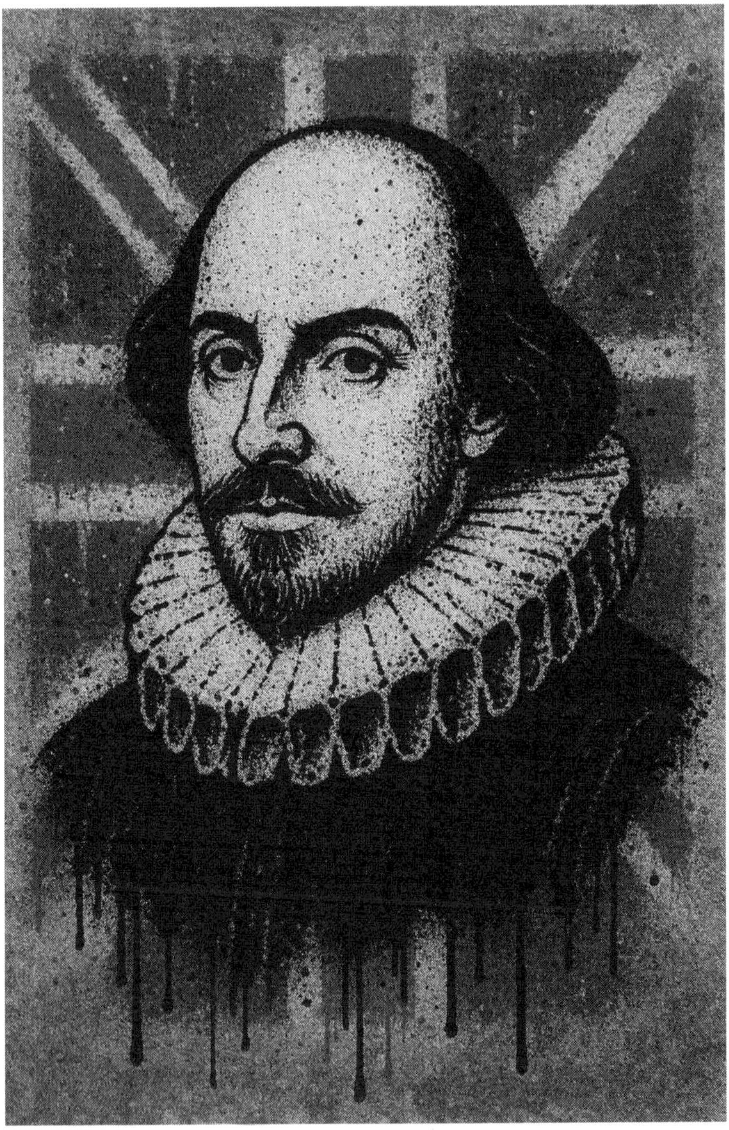

This isn't just a Twitter pile-on anymore. Cancel culture has slithered into the boardroom, the staffroom, and the HR department, cloaked in DEI jargon and 'sensitivity workshops.' Speak plainly, and you're 'problematic,' 'unsafe,' or, my favourite, 'not aligned with company values.' Never mind that those values twist like a weathervane in a storm. It's in hiring practices, company policies, medical guidelines, and sermons diluted to avoid ruffling feathers. It's the spirit of fear whispering, "Don't speak," just as you're about to say something real.

God didn't give us a spirit of fear, but of power, love, and a sound mind. So how do you slay this blasphemous beast, bloated with virtue-signalling and puffed-up pride? You don't negotiate with the modern Sanhedrin. You call them out. You flip the tables. You stride into the cultural temple with the boldness of Christ, knowing that truth doesn't need permission to speak.

Cancel culture is just heresy hunting with new branding. The mobs swapped pitchforks for hashtags and anonymous complaints, but their game's the same: shame, exile, and enforced obedience through fear. The stocks are now public smear campaigns, workplace sanctions, and bank account freezes.

Perhaps the Biblical demons Baal, Molech, and Mammon have returned, dressed up in progressive piety? It's not hard to imagine this to be the case. It would certainly explain a lot.

Yet holy rebellion, defiant, joyful, and unapologetic, cuts through deception like a hot knife. Here's how you fight back, spiritual warriors:

Top Rebellion Tips

1. Refuse to Self-Censor

The mind is the battlefield and cancel culture's best trick is convincing you to muzzle yourself. Every time you hesitate to speak truth, they gain ground. Don't let them. Voltaire wrote through exile. Solzhenitsyn wrote through gulags. Paul and Silas sang in chains. Speak boldly. Truth doesn't flinch.

2. Mock the False Gods

Laughter is a divine weapon. Elijah roasted Baal's prophets, and we should roast the sacred cows of gender ideology, climate hysteria, and woke dogma. Ridicule exposes the absurd, humbles the proud, and pops the balloon of pomposity. Oscar Wilde quipped from prison. Swift sliced with satire. Cancel culture thrives on fear but withers under fearless joy.

3. Assemble the Remnant

You're not alone. The banned, blocked, and fired carry the flame. You're Esther before the king, saying, "If I perish, I perish." Find your tribe: the outlaws, misfits, and iron-spined men and lion-hearted women. Speak together. Pray together. Be the holy rebels.

4. Build Parallel Systems

The establishment doesn't care about liberty. Fine. We don't need their permission. We have divine authority. Start your own education networks, platforms, publications. Like the early Christians, we go underground if we must, but we never stop speaking. C.S. Lewis didn't beg for approval to proclaim truth. Christ didn't wait for the temple's green light. This is more than resistance, it's reformation.

5. Anchor in Faith

The most critical weapon is faith in a divine power for good. Cancel culture's chaos is no match for unshakable belief. Lean into that truth. It's your sword and shield. Start the rebel Substack. Red-pill the public in Parliament Square. Launch the underground paper. When the farce collapses (and it will) the smoke will clear, and we'll stand tall, heirs to a Kingdom that cannot be shaken.

So, when the thought police come knocking, and the woke Sanhedrin demands your silence, what do you do? You don't grovel. You don't whisper apologies to the horde. You stand firm, chin up, and belt out the truth like a hymn in a hurricane. Let them clutch their pearls and freeze your bank card. Your soul's not for sale. Every silent prayer nicked, every honest word smeared, is a badge of honour in this holy rebellion.

Keep praying, keep thinking, keep speaking. Flood the digital Tower of Babel with fearless joy. The light shines in the darkness.

For in the end, truth doesn't just win. It reigns.

Chapter 7 - Trigger Warnings

How the UN Engineered an Offended Nation

Trigger Warning: Contains Ideas!

You can always count on modern British education establishments (particularly universities) to miss the point entirely. We now live in a country where novels about censorship are being censored... to protect people from the trauma of reading about censorship!

We used to arm young people with knowledge. Now we arm them with disclaimers.

Here's a headline for you: over 1,000 trigger warnings have been slapped onto the works of Shakespeare, Dickens, Austen, Chaucer, and even The Bible across UK universities. Exeter has issued warnings on The Iliad and The Odyssey in case someone's delicate soul can't cope with themes like rape or mortality.

Over at the University of the West of England, students are being prepped for battle with more than 220 trigger warnings for Shakespeare alone. Not just for violence and mental health, but for that most terrifying of hazards: balloons popping!

At first glance, it all looks like classic student theatre. Hypersensitive young people demanding emotional nappies to make it through an English degree. But that's not the full story.

THOUGHTCRIME DOES NOT ENTAIL DEATH: THOUGHTCRIME IS DEATH.

GEORGE ORWELL
1984

These trigger warnings aren't the disease. They're the rash. The real infection runs deeper.

A clear indication of this is the bizarre allegiance many young people now have to government orthodoxies, to Big Pharma, even to war (when it suits). There's no real social justice movements which stick it to the man anymore. Not unless you want to be branded far-right or a conspiracy theorist.

For the last decade, British schools and universities have been marinating in Critical Theory. That unholy brew of Critical Race Theory, Queer Theory, Gender Ideology, and other abstract American imports we never asked for. The classroom is no longer a place to explore ideas. It's a battlefield of power dynamics, privilege, and oppression narratives. Students are taught to read literature not for beauty or truth, but to spot who's being oppressed and who needs cancelling.

The result? A generation trained to flinch. They're taught to see harm in everything, to recoil from challenge, and to demand protection from the rough edges of reality. Disagreement? That's violence. Discomfort? That's trauma. Shakespeare? He's basically a hate crime.

But this mass emotional meltdown didn't happen by accident. It wasn't homegrown. It wasn't even particularly British. It was engineered. Globally. And you can thank the United Nations for it.

That's right. Your teenager's trigger warning on Great

Expectations can be traced back to a bunch of diplomats and development wonks in Geneva. DEI (Diversity, Equity, and Inclusion - for the uninitiated) isn't some quirky HR fad. It's a global doctrine, hardwired into the UN's Sustainable Development Goals (SDGs). This is not a side dish. It's the main course.

Here's how they've done it:

1. SDG 4 demands 'inclusive and equitable education.' Translation: tear down traditional standards and rebuild the system around identity politics.

2. SDG 5 (Gender Equality) and SDG 10 (Reduced Inequalities) require state-sponsored virtue signalling in every lecture hall, staffroom, and seminar.

3. UN agencies like UNESCO, UNICEF, and UN Women churn out policy toolkits that would make Orwell blush. Redefining everything from curriculum content to toilet signage.

Universities, ever desperate to look 'global,' swallow it all wholesale, embedding DEI nonsense into courses on everything from physics to poetry.

And because this dogma comes wrapped in the halo of sustainability, it sails past scrutiny. After all, who wants to argue with 'equality'? Who wants to sound anti-progress?

So, the UN builds the scaffolding, the universities hang the bunting, and next thing you know, Chaucer's getting sensitivity-checked and drama students need counselling over Macbeth.

It's not a student movement. It's a soft power strategy dressed up as compassion. DEI is the ideological Trojan horse, and the UN rolled it right through the gates of academia while we were busy checking our privilege.

If you've ever wondered how we ended up in a world where Romeo and Juliet needs a health warning, or why a British university now offers workshops on 'decolonising sonnets,' the answer is simple:

Follow the funding. Follow the policy. Follow the SDGs.

Great Literary Works with Trigger Warnings

1984: The Instruction Manual for 2025

George Orwell didn't write 1984 as a suggestion, but apparently that's how academia read it. Some universities have now slapped trigger warnings on the book, claiming it might distress students. Of course, it bloody might. That was the whole point.

"If you want a picture of the future, imagine a boot stamping on a human face - forever." 1984, Orwell

Well, the boot's here, only now it's eco-friendly, made from vegan leather, and comes with a QR code linking to an inclusivity workshop.

Fahrenheit 451: The How-To Guide for Cancel Culture

Ray Bradbury warned us that books don't need to be burned if people are too scared to read them. And what did we do? We put Fahrenheit 451 on the naughty shelf for being 'emotionally intense.'

"There is more than one way to burn a book. And the world is full of people running about with lit matches." Bradbury

Now those people run publishing houses and diversity boards. They don't need matches, just a red pen, a grievance study degree, and a mild allergy to context.

The Handmaid's Tale: Banned by the People It Was Warning About

The Handmaid's Tale is one of the most banned books in modern America and flagged in the UK for being 'controversial.'

> *"Nolite te bastardes carborundorum."* Margaret Atwood
> (Translation: Don't let the bastards grind you down.)

Hard to do when the bastards are in HR and think critical thinking is a hate crime.

Little Brother: When Teen Rebels Become Public Enemy Number One

Cory Doctorow's Little Brother features teenagers resisting a surveillance state. A modern rebellion. A stand for civil liberties. And therefore... far too subversive for school. Wouldn't want the kids getting ideas.

> *"Never underestimate the determination of a kid who is time-rich and cash-poor."* Cory Doctorow

Especially if they've still got free will and haven't been taught to fear everything from the common cold to warm weather.

Brave New World: The Dopamine-Sprinkled Nightmare

Now to Aldous Huxley, who saw a future where people don't need to be oppressed by force. They'll be so distracted, medicated, and emotionally pampered that they won't even notice the tyranny.

"A really efficient totalitarian state would be one in which the all-powerful executive... controls a population of slaves who do not have to be coerced, because they love their servitude." Aldous Huxley, Brave New World

Sound familiar?

The Gulag Archipelago: Solzhenitsyn's Slap Across the Face

For those still under the illusion that censorship is a 'soft' issue, Aleksandr Solzhenitsyn has something for you. A man who spent years in Stalin's gulags because he wrote the wrong thing i.e., the truth.

"The simple step of a courageous individual is not to take part in the lie." Aleksandr Solzhenitsyn

We now read books the way children cross roads: in high-vis jackets, holding someone's hand, and being warned about absolutely everything except the actual danger. This is an attempt to put an end to dissent.

Why do you think the unelected elite at the UN have inspired the censorship of books about totalitarianism?

If books and ideas disturb you, good. That's why so many great works have been written.

To challenge us. To make us think critically. To inspire dissent.

Top Rebellion Tips

1. Start a 'Trigger Warning-Free' Book Club

Invite normal people (i.e. anyone who doesn't break out in hives over Dickens) to a book club with one rule: No trigger warnings, no apologies, no sensitivity readers. Just bloody good stories. Serve wine, read *Lolita*, and watch the ghost of Orwell smile.

Call it 'The Offence Club' and make every meeting a safe space for dangerous ideas. Put Voltaire on the flyers. And don't forget to livestream the bits that make DEI officers twitch.

2. Trigger the Trigger-Happy with a T-Shirt

Sometimes the best protest is wearable. Create a line of T-shirts with slogans like:

- **'Warning: May Contain Opinions'**
- **'Safe Space? I Thought This Was Britain'**
- **'I Read Books Without Adult Supervision'**

Go one further: wear them to your old uni's open day. Walk into the DEI office and ask them for a trigger warning about *common sense*. Film their response,

3. Read Banned Books Aloud - In Public

If Orwell gets a warning label, then make it your personal mission to read *1984* in the most offensive place possible, loudly. Train station? Perfect. Tesco queue? Even better. University campus? *Chef's kiss.*

Take a battered copy of *1984*, stand outside the BBC, and read it like you're auditioning for *Downton Abbey meets Les Misérables*. Bonus points if you shout, *"Ignorance is strength!"* every time a Tesla drives by. If security approaches, simply say, "Don't worry, I've brought my own trigger warning. It's called a spine."

4. You Are Not Fragile - You're British, Act Like It

You descend from people who survived Blitz bombings, rationed tea, and the emotional trauma of watching *EastEnders* at Christmas. You do not need a warning before reading *Macbeth*. If your ancestors could storm the beaches of Normandy without a content note, you can handle *Jane Eyre* without crying into your hummus.

Next time someone offers you a trigger warning, offer them a biscuit and say, *"Thanks love, but I'll risk emotional growth."* Then walk off humming the Dad's Army theme like the unbothered legend you are.

Chapter 8 - The War on Childhood

Drag Queen Story Time and Other Nightmares They Forgot to Run by Your Nan

Once upon a time, childhood was about scraped knees, half-built dens in the woods, and being told to 'get on with it' when you cried over spilt milk.

Fast forward to now, and we're handing out chest binders like house points at Hogwarts and letting men in fishnets read 'gender diverse fairytales' to toddlers in public libraries.

Once a place for storybooks and silence, the local library has now become a theatre of ideological absurdity. And it's all in the name of 'inclusion.'

Let's be clear: there's nothing inclusive about dismantling a child's innocence before they can even tie their own shoelaces. We used to teach children the difference between right and wrong. Now we're teaching them how to 'explore their gender identity' before they've learned long division.

And where, might I ask, is Granny in all this? If someone tried to talk to your nan about 'age-appropriate kink education,' she'd clout them with her handbag and call the police. Quite right too.

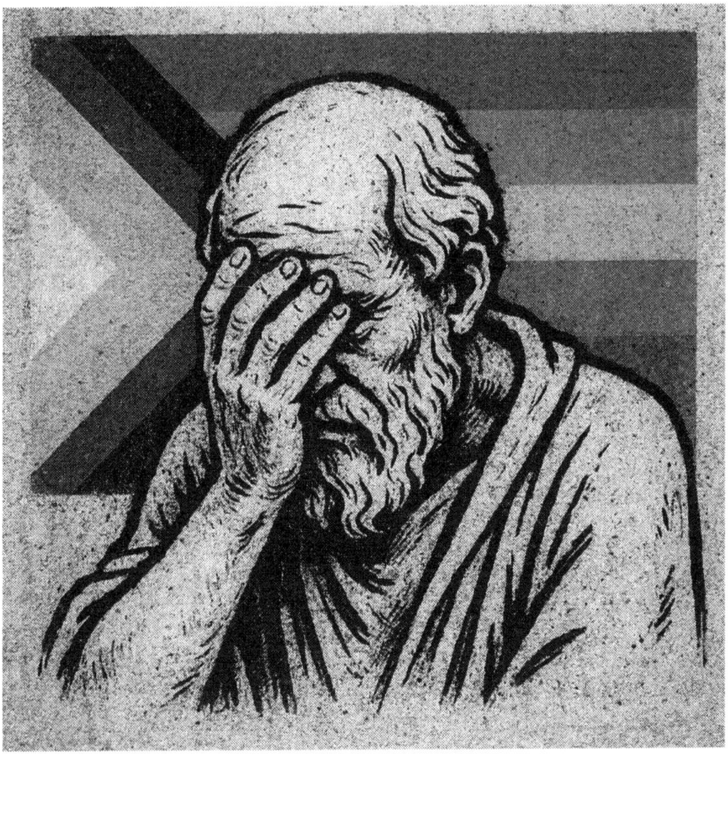

But today, it's parents who get reported to social services for saying, "Boys don't have periods." We've not just lost the plot, we've thrown the whole book in the bonfire and replaced it with a leaflet from Stonewall.

Socrates Would Be Cancelled

Socrates, the great gadfly of Athens, spent his days asking awkward questions. "What is justice?" "What is virtue?" "Are you sure your beliefs stand up to scrutiny?" Try that at a school board meeting today and you'll be shouted down by a woman with blue hair.

We're not educating children anymore; we're indoctrinating them.

The Socratic method was about critical thinking, not critical theory. It was about sharpening the mind, not softening it with safe spaces and trigger warnings. Socrates taught his pupils how to think, not what to think. He was executed for corrupting the youth. Ironically, this is the very thing our institutions are doing now, only with far less philosophical rigour and far more glitter.

If you were to wander into a modern classroom with a copy of Treasure Island or The Adventures of Tom Sawyer, you'd be accused of promoting 'colonial narratives.' The very stories that once taught boys to be brave, to question authority, and to do what is right, even when it's hard, are now on the chopping block.

The Erasure of Grit

Classic British literature used to be the backbone of moral education. Think of Kipling's *If*, that brilliant ode to resilience and stoicism. Could you imagine reading that aloud in today's classroom? You'd be hauled in front of the headteacher for 'toxic masculinity.'

But Kipling knew what we've forgotten: life is hard. You don't get through it by whining about pronouns.

Or consider Jane Eyre. A girl who refuses to submit to the expectations of her time, yet does so with integrity, self-respect, and moral clarity. She doesn't need to change her gender or scream into a TikTok filter to find herself. She grows through struggle. She learns the difference between passion and principle. She thinks. Imagine that!

Even Roald Dahl, patron saint of childhood rebellion, is getting a posthumous censorship courtesy of sensitivity readers. Apparently, words like 'fat' and 'ugly' are now hate speech. Well, guess what? The Trunchbull was fat and ugly, and that's what made her terrifying. Kids aren't stupid. They understand metaphor. They understand villainy. Or at least, they did, before we started wrapping everything in cotton wool and pumping their heads full of postmodern mush.

Grooming with a Rainbow Badge

Let's not mince words. When grown adults are having

conversations with primary school children about kink, sexual orientation, or how to chemically halt puberty, that's not education. That's grooming. The rainbow badge doesn't make it OK. It just makes it more insidious.

We've replaced biology with ideology. A teacher can't say, "Boys have penises," without fearing disciplinary action, but they're encouraged to host workshops on 'queer pleasure mapping' for children barely out of nappies. This isn't progress.

Back in the day, 'Sex Ed' meant awkwardly watching a VHS with cartoon sperm and being told not to get anyone pregnant before your GCSEs. Now it means being asked if you feel like a boy, girl, both, or neither, at age seven. Seven! At that age, I thought I was Dr. Spock. Thankfully, no one offered me surgery to make it official.

Time to Say No

We are raising a generation that knows their pronouns but not their multiplication tables. They can identify microaggressions but not propaganda. The classics taught children to strive for virtue, to embrace difficulty, to question the world without cynicism. That's what education is supposed to be. Instead, we've handed over the curriculum to activists with an axe to grind.

The time for polite disagreement is over. Parents must say no. Grandparents must say no. Teachers with a spine must say no.

This isn't about tolerance. It's about defending childhood from ideological colonisation. From the state. From corporations.

It's time we taught kids that life isn't about affirmation. It's about aspiration. That being uncomfortable is often the first step toward wisdom.

Your grandad stormed Normandy. Your son's being taught about chest binders. The time has come for a revolution within education.

Top Rebellion Tips

1. Start a 'Real Story Time' Movement: Nan Reads Kipling, Not Karen in a Corset

Let's reclaim the library from the glitter brigade. Drag queens out, Nans in. Bring your own flask, a dog-eared copy of *Treasure Island*, and a tray of homemade rock cakes. Real stories, real values, and no chance of anyone twerking in six-inch heels in front of your toddler.

2. Teach Your Kids the Art of Taking the Piss... Before Someone Takes Their Mind

Arm your children with sarcasm. Raise them to smell nonsense from 50 yards, and to ask, "Why?" every time someone with purple hair tells them boys can menstruate. Make satire their superpower.

3. Gatecrash the Next School Board Meeting Dressed as the Trunchbull

Drag queens are invited into schools? Fine. Two can play that game. Arrive in full *Matilda* villain gear, demand discipline, and read *If* by Kipling in your best Thatcher voice. Watch as the room breaks into nervous applause and quiet sobbing.

4. Start a Guerrilla 'Un-Woke Curriculum' And Make It Cooler Than Their TikTok Trash

Design your own underground syllabus: Shakespeare, Kipling, Greek myths, *Top Gear reruns*, proper history (with actual wars, not feelings). Run weekend sessions in your shed, church hall, or pub garden if you must.

So, here's to childhood. The real kind. Muddy-kneed, wide-eyed, gloriously innocent. The kind where fairytales stay magical, not ideological. Where boys climb trees, girls build forts, and nobody tells them they were born in the wrong body before they've lost their first tooth.

This isn't just a battle over books, or pronouns, or who gets to read a story in a library. It's a battle for the soul of the next generation. And if we don't stand up now, with courage, with clarity, with a bloody good sense of humour, we'll wake up in a country where kids are taught everything *except* how to be human.

So, stand your ground. Be the voice that says, "No," when everyone else is whispering, "Maybe." Say it with pride. Say it with humour. Say it with love.

Because one day, your child will look back and say, *"Thank God my mum and dad didn't let a bloke in a corset tell me who I was."*

And that, my friend, is the story worth telling. No trigger warnings required.

Chapter 9 - Immigration and Border Betrayal

Open Borders, Empty Promises, and the Great British Gaslighting

Let's begin with a spot of clarity, shall we? Legal immigration is not the problem.

My own wife's family came to Britain in the 1970s. Indians from East Africa, legally, respectfully, and with a work ethic that would make most career politicians look like they're permanently on annual leave. They integrated, contributed, and never once demanded to rewrite the national anthem. My late father in law (a completely blind master musician who worked seven days a week) was awarded an MBE by the Queen for his contributions.

That's the kind of immigration that adds to Britain's cultural tapestry.

But what we're dealing with now is something quite different.

I'm not talking about refugees fleeing war with nothing but the clothes on their backs and a desperate hope for safety. Britain has always opened its doors to the persecuted. Our track record there is one of our proudest. We took in Jews fleeing Hitler, and Asians expelled by Idi Amin. We *are* a nation of sanctuary when

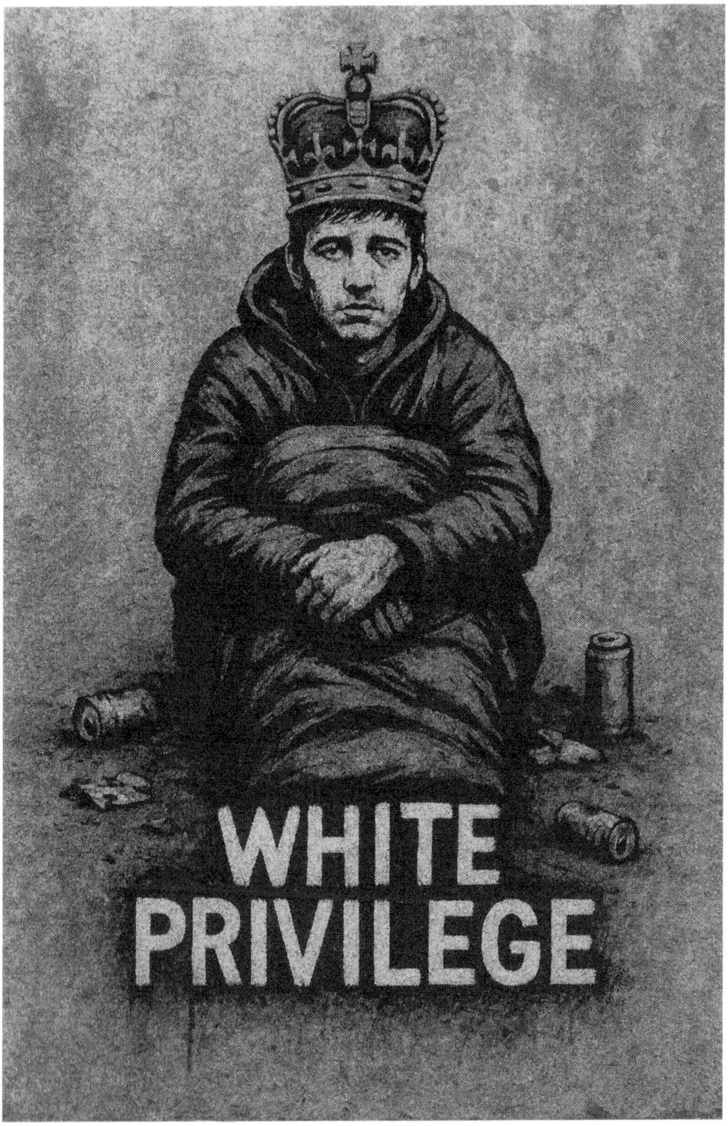
WHITE
PRIVILEGE

it matters.

But we also have to know the difference between someone escaping terror and someone escaping passport control.

Because right now, our southern coast is starting to resemble Heathrow's Terminal 5, if Terminal 5 had no check-in desk and no ID checks.

As of June 2025, over 20,000 people have already crossed the Channel in small boats this year alone. Just in one day in May, nearly 1,000 arrived.

Now, there are those who are undoubtedly genuine asylum seekers. Desperate people from broken countries, willing to risk their lives for safety and a stable future. Those individuals deserve our compassion, care, and fair processing.

But let's be honest, a good chunk of these arrivals aren't women and children fleeing for their lives. They are men aged between 18–39, but with well-rehearsed stories and apparently zero fear of British immigration enforcement. The Home Office has acknowledged that some asylum seekers have arrived with extremist sympathies.

In countries like Afghanistan and parts of Iraq or Syria, women often live under harsh patriarchal or theocratic rule. These societies may treat women as subordinate, restrict education, force veiling, permit child marriage, or deny legal rights. Men from these backgrounds arrive with these deeply entrenched ideological leanings.

Call it what you like, 'irregular arrivals,' 'asylum seekers,' or 'unexpected visitors,' but the sheer number of undocumented men in their twenties landing daily would make a national service recruiter weep with joy.

We now spend £8 million a day housing illegal arrivals. More than the annual NHS dentistry budget. And with over 400 hotels in use, entire seaside towns are starting to feel like they're hosting an endless international student exchange. Except no one leaves.

And while real British veterans are roughing it on pavements with sleeping bags and bad knees, some of these new arrivals are Instagramming buffet breakfasts from Radissons and Novotels. It's not xenophobic to say: something's gone a bit pear-shaped.

Prominent non-white voices are speaking up too. Kemi Badenoch has defended British values and warned against importing ideologies that clash with equality and freedom. Yasmin Alibhai-Brown has cautioned against mass migration without integration. Kenan Malik has argued that immigration must respect the foundations of liberal democracy. And filmmaker Sonita Gale has exposed the dysfunction of the current system. These are British citizens from culturally diverse backgrounds who value fairness, security, and sovereignty. Just like the rest of us.

Now, some will say, "Be kind. Show compassion." And they're absolutely right. But kindness requires discernment. Real compassion isn't a free-for-all. It's not giving everyone who turns up in a dinghy a Premier Inn keycard and a benefits guide. It's helping those in need, *not those gaming the system.*

Because the truth is, this isn't accidental. This is system failure by design. Our politicians couldn't organise a border policy in a sandcastle competition.

But the open borders chaos goes deeper than Westminster. There are powerful forces behind this global game of musical borders.

The United Nations, for one, has made no secret of its goal to 'facilitate regular and safe migration' under the *Global Compact for Migration.* Sounds harmless enough, until you realise it basically translates to: 'Let's make mass movement of people permanent and policy-proof.'

And then there's George Soros, the billionaire who apparently never met a border he didn't want to dismantle. He once wrote that:

> "Sovereignty is an obstacle to global governance. Migration is one of the engines to reshape society."

Lovely. Because nothing says 'democracy' like unelected billionaires reshaping entire cultures from the comfort of their private jet.

Through his Open Society Foundations, Soros has funded countless NGOs and lobbying groups that push open border ideology across Europe. Call it philanthropy, call it social engineering, either way, it's not being voted on by the British public.

The big idea? That borders are outdated relics. That nation-states are selfish. That mass migration is both inevitable and virtuous. And anyone who disagrees must be either backward or bigoted, or both.

The United Nations claims it's all about 'safe, orderly, and regular migration,' But their *Global Compact for Migration* calls on nations to 'enhance the availability and flexibility of pathways for regular migration' while simultaneously urging them to 'promote the dignity and rights of all migrants, regardless of migration status.' Why? Because this paves the way for digital ID (their solution).

The political class cheers from gated communities and Westminster wine bars. And it's working-class Brits who pay the price. Overstretched schools, endless GP queues, housing shortages, and a creeping sense that the country they grew up in is being quietly rewritten.

Because a nation that can't control its borders isn't a nation. It's a travel agency with an identity crisis.

And let's not pretend this is just an economic or humanitarian issue. It's also a matter of national security. You don't need to be James Bond to see that when your coastline is more porous than a sponge in a monsoon, bad actors will exploit it. Even MI5 has warned that some arrivals have been flagged with extremist sympathies.

We've already seen ISIS sympathisers, al-Qaeda fanboys, and

suspected spies arrive on our shores with no documents, no history, and no intention of embracing British values.

This isn't just a migration crisis. It's a border betrayal. Britain doesn't need more slogans; it needs sovereignty. And it certainly doesn't need compassion lectures from people who double-lock their doors at night and head off to Glastonbury, where the site is ringed by a 12-foot steel perimeter fence, patrolled by security, with strict entry controls and prosecution for trespassers. You breach that, you don't get a welcome pack. You get removed, fined, or arrested. Funny how border control is perfectly acceptable when it's for a music festival, but somehow oppressive when it's for a country.

What Britain needs now is courage, clarity, and honesty.

Because behind all the chaos, there's a wizard behind the curtain, and it's not Gandalf, it's George Soros with a cheque book and a Messiah complex. The man's spent more money meddling in national identities than most countries spend defending theirs. And his open-border philosophy has seeped through global institutions like red wine through a white sofa.

Then there's the United Nations, waddling in with the moral authority of a traffic warden at a Formula 1 race, telling sovereign nations they must accommodate 'regular and safe migration' which is code for: *Sit down, shut up, and let Brussels and Davos decide who lives on your street.*

Britain is not a social experiment. It's a nation. With borders, history, and values. Legal immigration is a strength of Britain. Illegal immigration is a weakness.

We lock our front doors at night for a reason. Yet somehow suggesting the nation do the same is now 'far-right.' This creates division, racial tensions, and national security risks. All by design, of course, and with no real compassion or thought for genuine asylum seekers.

A country without borders is just a postcode with a flag. Britain deserves better than that.

Top Rebellion Tips

1. When the authorities come up with digital ID as the solution - reject it

We've got Brits being fined for driving five miles over the limit, but 25-year-old blokes with no passports, no papers, and suspiciously fresh trainers are welcomed like long-lost cousins. You try flying to Benidorm without ID and see how far you get.

Next time you get asked for ID at the bank, just say, *"I'm undocumented, but with lived experience,"* and see what happens. Or go full satire and try boarding a plane in a rubber dinghy.

2. Our Asylum System Moves Slower Than a Sunday Roast in Slippers

The backlog's so bad you could *apply* for asylum, get a law degree, *become* a Home Office caseworker, and still not see your file processed.

Send a potato to the Home Office and label it: *'Speed Consultant.'* Because frankly, even root veg moves faster than our asylum decisions. Put up posters: 'Apply Now. Results Expected by 2099!'

3. Celebrities Want Open Borders. As Long As It's Not Near Their Pilates Studio

It's always the same crowd. Actors, musicians, media people calling everyone racist from Notting Hill townhouses with blackout blinds and private schools. They cry 'let them in' from behind curtains and keep their own postcodes more exclusive than a Soho House toilet. Create a *'Host-a-Migrant'* challenge for virtue-signalling celebs. You say open borders are lovely? Great. Here's a bunk bed and a bloke who's got six phones and no surname. Let's see how *inclusive* you feel after a week.

4. We Put More Effort into Eurovision Security Than Our Borders

When Eurovision comes to town, it's patrolled like a nuclear summit. One bloke sneezes wrong and MI5's on him. But 1,000 men can land on the coast unannounced, and they're asked if they'd prefer a room with Wi-Fi or sea view.

CANCEL THIS

Write to your MP and ask if we can outsource border protection to Glastonbury security. Apparently they're better at vetting tents than the Home Office is at vetting terror suspects.

5. Plenty of Black and Asian Brits Are Saying It Too. But the Media Pretends They Don't Exist

You won't hear it on the BBC, but many Black and Asian Brits. who were born in Britain or arrived legally, worked hard, and built lives, are just as fed up with the border chaos as everyone else. They're watching the system get abused while being told to stay quiet in case someone gets offended.

They know that uncontrolled immigration isn't 'inclusive' it's unfair. It undermines the people who played by the rules and disrespects the values they embraced when they made Britain home.

Next time someone calls you heartless for wanting border control, say: *"Tell that to my parents, who filled out every form, paid every fee, and waited years to get here legally."* Then quote Kemi Badenoch, Trevor Phillips, or Sonita Gale.

We are not a hateful nation. We are a fair nation. And fairness means knowing the difference between a refugee and a rule-breaker. Between compassion and chaos. Between a nation of sanctuary, and a nation taken for a ride.

This isn't about race. It's about respect. It's about protecting the people who did it right. The mums and dads who queued at embassies, filled out endless paperwork, worked two jobs, raised kids who call Britain home. It's about honouring their effort, not mocking it with a broken system that rewards those who skip the line.

Let this be the moment where we stop apologising for common sense. Where we stop nodding along with the madness. Where we rise, not in rage, but in resolve.

Britain's borders are more open than a Love Island contestant's DMs, and about as well thought through. Meanwhile, British pensioners need six forms of ID just to book a GP appointment and a blood oath to get a hip replacement.

We have a right to say no. To demand secure borders. To demand that sovereignty means something. And to say it without being slurred, smeared, or silenced.

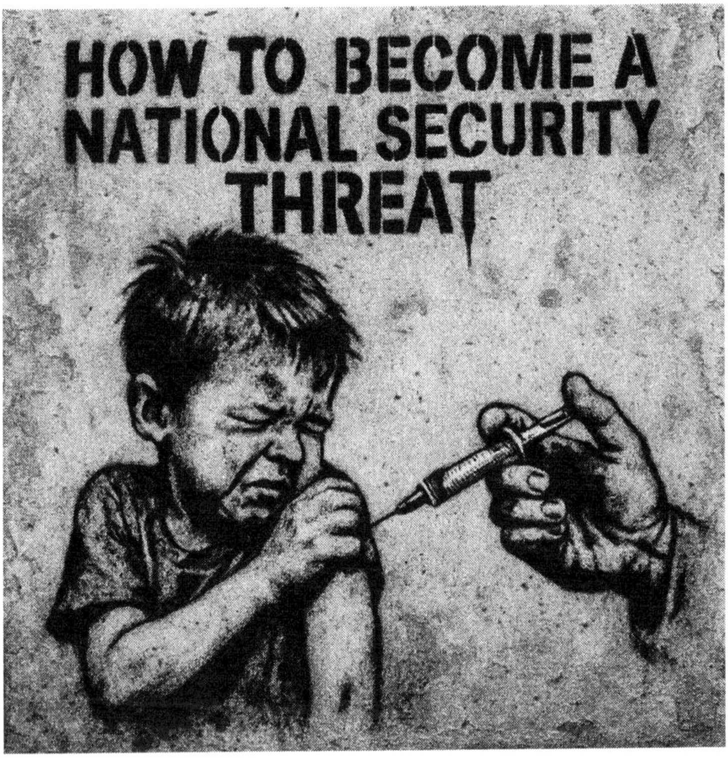
HOW TO BECOME A
NATIONAL SECURITY
THREAT

Chapter 10 - Digital ID

You'll Own Nothing and Scan Everything

Welcome to Brave New Blighty, where your papers are digital, your wallet is monitored, and your freedom is conditional. Great Britain is teetering on the brink of ushering in a national digital ID system.

Yes, the same Britain that once prided itself on civil liberties, privacy, and a general disdain for government overreach. Now, our political class, like a dodgy Carry On character with a penchant for surveillance, is dangling the shiny promise of 'convenience' while quietly sliding the handcuffs into place.

Think back, if your memory hasn't been wiped by the Ministry of Health. During the pandemic, we got a taste of digital control with those charming little vaccine passports. Want to enter a venue? Flash your app. Want to fly, work, or exist in polite society? Better have your QR code scanned, jab status verified, and obedience levels recalibrated.

That little COVID experiment was a not-so-dry run for a far more sinister project.

The digital ID being proposed is not some benign bit of modern admin. It is, quite frankly, a blueprint for technocratic control. It won't stop with your name and date of birth. Oh no. Soon, your biometric data, spending habits, health records, social media activity, and ideological alignment could be packed into your shiny new BritCard.

Want to buy a pint or a sausage roll? Better scan in first. Had too many pints this week? Sorry, your cholesterol's high and your carbon credits are low. Try again next month.

Now imagine the government deciding you've said something 'hateful' (which is Newspeak for 'unpopular'). Suddenly, your car won't start. Your social media is locked. Your travel rights revoked. This is not a stretch of the imagination. This is a roadmap, and we're already halfway there.

During the COVID era, the Canadian government showed us what financial control looks like in real time: freezing the bank accounts of protesters and their supporters with the flick of a bureaucratic switch. Here in Britain, the Public Authorities (Fraud, Error, and Recovery) Bill is quietly being pushed through to give similar powers to our own institutions. Banks would be compelled to monitor accounts using secret government criteria. We already have 'non-crime hate incidents' logged by the police. So why not tag your digital ID with a bit of extra social suspicion?

This isn't sci-fi. It's not even speculative fiction. It's the logical conclusion of a government drunk on power and corporations only too happy to do their bidding. Because only the government can coerce the private sector into compliance, and with digital ID, that coercion becomes seamless. Whether it's PayPal, your bank, or your local supermarket, compliance will be built in.

Let's not forget that digital ID isn't just a British pet project. Globally, the trend is full steam ahead. The EU is rolling out its own European Digital Identity Wallet (EUDI), a cheerful acronym masking a bureaucratic leviathan. In the US, Palantir (a name that sounds like it should belong to Sauron's Rolodex) is busy building data-integration platforms so powerful even its former engineers have sounded the alarm. It's digital ID in everything but name.

And what follows digital ID? That delightful invention from dystopia: the social credit system. Say something wrong. Think something unapproved. Donate to the wrong cause. Suddenly you're locked out of your finances, denied access to transport, and treated like a digital leper. Welcome to 1984 with a user interface.

Of course, the BBC and The Guardian have done their bit to label any such concerns as 'conspiracy theories.' According to them, worrying about surveillance, control, or globalist agendas is just paranoid nonsense. BBC Verify will explain, ever so patiently, that central bank digital currencies and digital ID schemes are perfectly safe and anyone who disagrees probably owns too many tinfoil hats.

The Guardian, never one to miss a chance to condescend, dismisses opposition as the whining of anti-globalist populists. Apparently, if you oppose vaccine passports or a national ID scheme, you're only a hop and a goose-step away from the far right. The new mantra: trust the institutions, question nothing, comply.

But even as the media scoffs, the examples of control keep piling up. PayPal has become the financial enforcer of woke orthodoxy. In the UK, it suspended accounts belonging to the Free Speech Union, The Daily Sceptic, and Toby Young for the crime of expressing lockdown scepticism. After a public backlash, they reinstated them, but the message was clear: step out of line, lose your money. Even parents' group UsForThem was targeted for daring to question school closures.

In the US, PayPal went further, banning Gays Against Groomers for challenging gender ideology in schools, and cutting off biologist Colin Wright for the heresy of believing in biological sex. If private companies can do this now, imagine what they'll do once plugged into a national digital ID grid.

For now, you can still talk about digital ID without being entirely cancelled. But the window is closing. Soon, questioning the BritCard will be seen as dangerous extremism, lumped in with flat-Earthers and anti-vaxxers, and probably flagged on some AI-run government watchlist.

Thankfully, not everyone is asleep at the digital wheel. Groups like Big Brother Watch, Open Rights Group, Privacy International, and the Free Speech Union are sounding the alarm. UsForThem continues to champion parental rights and bodily autonomy. Even former Cabinet Minister and Brexit bulldog Lord David Frost has called digital ID 'deeply illiberal' and warned of its threat to personal freedom. Once dismissed as fringe cranks, these voices are now at the vanguard of defending the very concept of liberty.

So, what's the solution? It's simple. Don't comply. Don't sign up. Don't hand over your data to a government that has shown time and again it cannot be trusted. If enough people say 'no,' the whole rotten edifice collapses.

Aldous Huxley warned of a future where people are enslaved by pleasure and convenience. Orwell warned of a boot stamping on a human face forever. Yevgeny Zamyatin, in *We*, painted a vision of a society so ordered, so controlled, that citizens were numbers, not names. Digital ID is the lovechild of all three.

The next time someone offers you a seamless, secure, government-approved identity wallet, remember: the price of convenience might just be your freedom. Cancel the BritCard before it cancels you.

Top Rebellion Tips

1. Say No to Digital ID. Your Nan Didn't Fight the Blitz So You Could Be Barcoded at Greggs

Seriously. We used to fight tyranny with Spitfires. Now we're surrendering to it via smartphone app. If Churchill saw this lot scanning in for sausage rolls, he'd slap them with his cigar.

Refuse to scan anything. If the government wants your data,

make them earn it: in handwriting, on paper, with a leaky biro and your worst spelling.

2. Keep Cash in Your Pocket Like It's a Loaded Weapon. Because One Day It Might Be

They can't cancel what they can't track. You pay with cash, and suddenly you're the only person in Tesco *not* on MI5's 'Said Something Sarcastic Online' list.

Start paying for everything in coins, preferably jangling loose change like a disobedient granddad at the pub. Announce loudly: *"Sorry, I don't do QR codes. I do the King's face."*

3. If You Need a QR Code to Buy a Pint, It's Not a Country, It's a Prison with Tap Water

Nothing says freedom quite like having to *digitally prove your existence* to order chips. Next they'll be locking the bogs unless you've got a carbon credit and a government-approved opinion.

So, chin up, Britain. Rip up the QR codes, pay in cash, and tell the data-sniffers to sod off. We didn't survive world wars, ration books, and fifteen seasons of *Strictly Come Dancing* just to be reduced to a blinking dot on a government dashboard. We are not a nation of scannable sheep. We are bulldogs in Barbour jackets, and it's time we bit back.

Chapter 11 - The Death of Satire

When Monty Python Is Offensive and Comedy Gets Cancelled

There was a time when Britain was the home of savage wit. The land of Oscar Wilde's flamboyant zingers, Churchill's bulldog one-liners, and the glorious, surreal absurdity of *Monty Python*. We didn't just tolerate satire, we sharpened it like a bayonet and pointed it at everything. The monarchy, the government, the clergy, the French. No one was safe. That was the whole bloody point.

Now we've got diversity panels determining whether a sketch about a man with a silly walk might be ableist. "This programme contains language and attitudes of its time," the BBC solemnly intones before rerunning *Fawlty Towers*, like we're all children about to be traumatised by Basil mentioning the war.

Satire hasn't just died, it's been garrotted in a back alley by a gang of Twitter activists wielding hashtags and master's degrees in grievance studies.

Satire is supposed to offend. It's meant to cut, to provoke, to make you uncomfortable enough to actually *think*. It's not supposed to be a warm hug from your therapist. It's the scathing teacher at the back of the pub who tells you you're talking bollocks, and your trousers are too tight. That's comedy.

DEFEND YOUR KIDS

We used to be able to laugh at ourselves. That's what made British humour legendary. Self-deprecation with a teaspoon of sarcasm and a punch of absurdity. Think of *Yes, Minister*, *Blackadder*, *Spitting Image*, even *Little Britain* in its gloriously unhinged heyday. Not a safe space in sight. And thank God for it.

But the rot didn't stop at telly or stage. It's infected the streets too. Because now it's not just the comedians being cancelled. It's *you*. The average bloke or lass trying to survive another shift without tripping over an HR policy. You used to be able to crack a joke in the office, down the pub, or while waiting for a delayed train without being hauled in for re-education.

Not anymore!

Try a bit of banter at work and suddenly it's 'inappropriate conduct.' Say something sarcastic in the break room and someone's filed it with HR before you've finished your biscuit. If you dare use irony on a Zoom call, someone's already clipped it and uploaded it to LinkedIn with a caption about 'toxic workplace culture.'

The modern workplace isn't a hive of productivity. It's a hostage situation where everyone's terrified of having a laugh and expressing an opinion. Laughter has been replaced by that awkward fake chuckle people do when they're not sure if they're allowed to laugh. The kind of strangled noise you'd expect from someone on their deathbed.

And the pub? The last surviving arena of free speech, now under siege from all sides. What used to be a sacred space for brutal banter and merciless ribbing is now crawling with undercover offence archaeologists. People mining your every pint-fuelled sentence for microaggressions. Crack the wrong joke and you're a 'bigot.' Make fun of your mate's bald head and suddenly you've committed follicular hate speech.

We used to treasure our pub philosophers. The sarcastic, boozy prophets of nonsense who could turn a political scandal into a punchline. They were our public intellectuals. Now they're being replaced by people who start sentences with, "As someone who identifies as..." and end them with absolutely nothing funny.

On the street, humour is just as endangered. The British ability to survive any horror (war, queues, rail strikes, losing the Ashes) relied on gallows humour. But now you can be arrested for saying the wrong thing *online*, let alone on a park bench. Police have shown up at people's doors for memes. Actual memes. Imagine George Orwell hearing that.

We've turned the entire country into a humourless HR seminar. We've outsourced our sense of irony to tech platforms and tribunals. The Great British Public, once world leaders in sarcasm, understatement, and the comedic side-eye, is now too nervous to speak plainly for fear of saying something 'problematic.'

The truth is, the public is funnier than most modern comedians. Always has been. The cabbie with a one-liner about the government. The builder who turns throwing the fucks into a performance art. The old lady who could drop a sharper insult in five words than any Guardian columnist could in five thousand. That's our heritage.

This is not just about jokes. It's about freedom. The freedom to be irreverent. The freedom to mock, tease, exaggerate, ridicule, and play with language. These aren't just luxuries. They're tools of dissent. And that's precisely why they're being smothered. You control humour, you control speech. You control speech, you control thought.

Authoritarians loathe satire. They hate it because it exposes the absurdity of their power. Satire doesn't respect their sacred cows. It slaughters them, roasts them, and serves them with gravy. That's why our rulers love 'misinformation' laws and 'online harms' bills, not to protect the vulnerable, but to protect *themselves* from mockery.

We need to uncancel the public. We need to restore the art of the cheeky comment, the sly innuendo, the dry one-liner that confuses Americans. We need to make it *safe to be funny* again. Not just on stage, but in the office, the pub, the family WhatsApp chat, and yes, even Twitter (or whatever Elon's calling it this week).

Because if we can't take the piss, we're doomed to be ruled by those who can't take a joke. And frankly, they're the ones who need it most.

Top Rebellion Tips

1. Carry a Disclaimer Sign That Reads: 'Warning: May Contain Jokes'

Use it in meetings, family gatherings, and funerals if necessary. If Monty Python needs a warning label, so do you. Especially when mocking management or your vegan nephew's pronouns for his pet rabbit.

2. Turn Offence Into a Competitive Sport: First to Flinch Loses

Gather your mates and see who can deliver the most inappropriate joke in a safe space without being cancelled. Bonus points if someone from marketing reports you to HR before pudding.

3. Host a 'Cancelled Comedy Night' in the Pub.

Put *Fawlty Towers*, *Little Britain*, and *Brass Eye* on a loop. Serve pints. If anyone says, "That's problematic," offer them a colouring book and directions to the nearest TED Talk.

4. Quote Shakespeare at Work Until Someone Reports You for Microaggressions

Start every meeting with, "Methinks the lady doth protest

too much," and watch HR panic over whether you've just misgendered Susan from Finance. Bonus points if you slip in, "Out, damned woke spot!" during diversity training.

So, here's the plan, Britain: put your pith helmet on, sharpen your wit, and start offending the right people again. Mock the madness, laugh at the lunatics, and for God's sake, take the piss like your freedom depends on it, because it bloody well does.

Satire isn't dead. It's just been locked in the loo with a diversity officer banging on the door. Time to kick it down, rescue the punchlines, and remind the world what Britain stands for. The land of hope and glory.

I MUST CREATE A SYSTEM,
OR BE ENSLAVED BY
ANOTHER MAN'S;
WILLIAM BLAKE

Chapter 12 - Questioning Medical Interventions

From Puberty Blockers to Covid-19 Vaccines

(*Or how to become a national security threat*)

In 2021, The Telegraph printed my comment:

> "I have a legal duty to safeguard and promote the welfare of children. I do not believe that we should ask healthy children to undergo a medical intervention with known risks where there is little or no benefit to them."

Well. You'd have thought I'd confessed to strangling kittens in Downing Street.

What followed? Three complaints. Three investigations. Cleared every time, by the way, and a complaint to the *Counter Extremism Division*. Because apparently, saying 'maybe don't inject kids with experimental drugs' is now one step below plotting a coup. I also got reported to *PREVENT*, the UK's anti-terror programme. Yep. Me, a dad, and a headmaster, labelled alongside ISIS because I questioned pharmaceutical experimentation on children.

Then came the covert monitoring by the Counter Disinformation

Unit (basically the Ministry of Truth, but with more spreadsheets), a complaint to *Ofsted*, and permanent exile from Twitter 1.0. All the complaints were anonymous, of course. Nothing says courage like trying to cancel someone from behind a gender-neutral keyboard while sipping an oat milk latte.

Yet not a single person, not one, has publicly challenged what I actually said. Because they can't. It's basic common sense. And it aged like a fine Merlot.

In May 2024, puberty blockers were *finally* banned in the UK. Cheers erupted from various politicians and celebrities. The same politicians and TV personalities who'd been mute for years suddenly popped up with, "I've always had concerns." But rewind six months and this was an off limits topic.

Why? Because nobody wants to be called a 'transphobe.' That's the magic spell. Say the T-word, and everyone gets up and leaves the room. Forget facts, forget ethics, forget protecting kids.

The NHS, was finally forced to admit the bleeding obvious, said in March 2024:

> "There is not enough evidence to support the safety or clinical effectiveness of puberty-suppressing hormones."

No shit, Sherlock. It only took how many broken families, destroyed futures and irreversible side effects?

But the bravery award doesn't go to politicians. It goes to the ones who spoke out *before* it was safe to do so. J.K. Rowling,

Allison Pearson, Molly Kingsley, Jordan Peterson. They dared to say, "Hang on a minute…" while the mob screamed for their heads. Now they're vindicated. But they were burned at the stake first.

It's important to acknowledge who we're up against. Big Pharma. The global cartel with better PR than the Royal Family and a rap sheet longer than Hunter Biden's WhatsApp messages.

Remember Pfizer's $2.3 billion fine in 2009? That wasn't for mislabelling vitamin C. They got caught marketing drugs for uses they knew were dangerous and in some cases, fatal. And yet we were told to trust the 'safe and effective' mantra.

Then there's the opioid crisis. Entire towns hollowed out like a post-pandemic high street because Big Pharma cooked up an addiction epidemic and sold it in blister packs. The Sackler family made billions pushing OxyContin. Then they donated to museums for good PR.

The same companies sponsor the World Health Organization and wine and dine half of Westminster while lobbying policies that coincidentally align with their profit margins.

Now enter COVID-19, stage left. Suddenly, the whole nation went into cult mode. The government wheeled out the 'Nudge Unit,' MI5, MI6, the 77th Brigade, and the RAF to monitor people like me for 'wrongthink.' Asking questions about lockdowns or school closures made you a public enemy. Questioning the jab made you an extremist. It was like living in a dystopian episode of *Black Mirror*, directed by SAGE and co-written by Matt Hancock's ego.

The same pattern repeats. Want to question gender ideology? You're an extremist. Not sold on climate apocalypse? Extremist. Concerned about illegal immigration? Bigot. Wave the Union Jack? Might as well burn a cross while you're at it.

It's become a political tactic. Brand anyone who deviates from the script as a threat to democracy. That way, no debate is needed. Just cancel, censor, and carry on.

However, it's *not British* to stay silent. We've always been a nation of sceptics and piss-takers. We invented satire. We survived two World Wars, the Spice Girls, and ten seasons of *Love Island*. We can survive this too. But only if we grow a spine and say, "Enough."

If we can't protect our kids from medical harm, from ideological indoctrination, from the ruthless profiteering of global corporations and cowardly politicians, then what the hell are we doing?

Hundreds of thousands, and perhaps millions of us, stood up during the Covid era. We still stand up today. And if that makes us extremists, then so be it. Because history has a funny way of proving yesterday's black sheep were right all along.

But here's the good news: the tide is turning. Slowly. Painfully. Like watching a tanker do a U-turn in the Suez Canal, but turning it is. Puberty blockers banned. Politicians backpedalling so fast they've worn holes in their Hush Puppies. And the public? They're not buying it anymore. Not the slogans, not the guilt trips, not the 'trust the experts' sermons from the same people who couldn't organise a vaccine fridge in a pharmacy.

And here's what they *really* hate: we're laughing at them now. That's the death blow to tyrants and technocrats. You can call us names, cancel our accounts, stick us on watchlists, and smear us in the press. But once we start laughing, you've lost the room.

Because nothing scares the joyless authoritarians more than humour. Especially British humour.

We are the descendants of people who survived the Blitz on nothing but sarcasm and spam. We built empires, lost them, shrugged, and made sitcoms about it. We can handle this bunch of pharmaceutical fanboys, ideology peddlers and digital despots.

The truth is, people are waking up. Parents are asking questions. Teachers are speaking out. Doctors are growing spines. Even comedians, those still clinging to their gonads, are beginning to joke about the things we were told we couldn't even *mention*. And that, my friends, is progress.

So don't despair. Don't back down. Don't hand over your common sense to the cult of 'inclusivity' when it's clearly excluding truth. Don't let them gaslight you into silence.

And if they come for you with anonymous complaints, government dossiers, or a visit from the Department of Wrongthink, don't flinch. In Britain, we don't bow to bullies.

CANCEL THIS

We mock them mercilessly. For the kids. For the truth. For the sheer bloody-minded joy of refusing to be told what to think.

Because in the end, the most rebellious, most British, most necessary act of all, is telling the truth and laughing while you do it.

Top Rebellion Tips

1. If the 'Experts' Were So Right, Why Are They All Backpedalling Like Boris on a Boris Bike?

Next time someone quotes 'the science,' just ask which episode we're on now. Season 1: *Trust the Jab.* Season 2: *Block the Puberty.* Season 3: *We Never Said That.* It's less medical advice; more Netflix box set for the clinically gullible.

2. Keep a Rolodex of Smug Cowards Now Claiming 'They Always Had Concerns'

When someone says, *"Well, in hindsight…"* hand them a mirror and a muzzle. If they were silent while kids got sterilised and schools became pharma playgrounds, they don't get to join the resistance now. They get to sit in the corner with a clipboard and think about their life choices.

3. Teach Your Kids the First Rule of Modern Medicine: If They Offer You a Lollipop After, Say No

Puberty blockers, hormone injections, mental health labels like Pokémon cards. This isn't healthcare. It's ideology in a lab coat. If your GP sounds like they trained on TikTok, it's time to switch to common sense.

4. When the Department of Wrongthink Comes Knocking, Offer Them Tea and a Copy of the Nuremberg Code

Tell them, cheerfully: *"Yes, I'm a domestic extremist. I believe in parental rights, bodily autonomy, and not injecting children with Big Pharma's latest profit margin."* Then wave them off with a smile and a middle finger in a sensible British mug.

The tide's shifting, the mask's slipped, and the lunatics running the lab are being dragged back to the waiting room. We're not just questioning the narrative anymore, we're rewriting it with better grammar, sharper jokes, and actual facts. The battle isn't over, but we've got truth on our side, sarcasm in our veins, and a national treasure called humour that no government agency can regulate.

So, crack a joke and keep speaking the truth. Because we're not going down at all. We're rising up, laughing louder, thinking sharper, and proving that in Britain, we'll defend our kids like modern-day warriors of Camelot, armed with facts, wit, and swords made of sarcasm.

So, chin up, you glorious extremist. The Round Table's got room for one more.

Chapter 13 - Rebellion: A British Tradition

From Boudica to Brexit: We've Always Told Tyrants to Sod Off

Let's get one thing straight: rebellion isn't some imported ideology from across the Atlantic or a TikTok trend with a hashtag and a dance. Rebellion is British. It's not just in our blood; it *is* our blood. It's tea thrown into harbours, angry letters penned by candlelight, battle cries from pub landlords after ten pints, and the great British pastime of telling anyone in authority to sod off.

You think cancel culture has teeth? Try living under Henry VIII. The man cancelled *wives*. We survived him. We survived the Normans. We survived Gordon Brown.

It started with Boudica, didn't it? The ultimate ginger rebel queen, standing up to the Romans because they thought they could barge into Britain, slap on a toga, and start collecting taxes without so much as a please or thank you. Boudica didn't write a sternly worded letter to the local MP. She burned down London. She's the original unsubtle protest.

Then there was the Magna Carta in 1215, when a bunch of pissed-off barons basically told King John, "Nah mate, you can't just nick our stuff because you're wearing a shiny hat."

BILL GATES OWNS FOUR PRIVATE JETS—TWO GULFSTREAM G650ERs AND TWO BOMBARDIER CHALLENGER 350s. HE ALSO HAS A 66,000 SQ FT MANSION IN MEDINA, WASHINGTON, PLUS LUXURY PROPERTIES IN FLORIDA AND A PRIVATE ISLAND IN BELIZE. NOT BAD FOR A GUY PREACHING CARBON FOOTPRINTS.

That little scroll was the beginning of holding power to account. It birthed the idea that even the bloke with the biggest crown wasn't above the law.

Fast forward to 1688. The Glorious Revolution. Glorious because we booted out one king, brought in another, and didn't even need a civil war. We pulled off regime change with more grace than an episode of *Bake Off*. That's how British rebellion works. With decorum *and* indignation.

We're the only people on earth who can simultaneously queue in silence *and* plot a full-blown cultural insurrection. We invented the humble revolution. Not the American kind, with muskets and melodrama, but the sort where you get the job done, then go home and make a cup of tea.

Rebellion has always been about protecting the ordinary Brit from the overreaching elite. Whether it's Charles I getting the chop for being too divine for his own boots or the peasants of 1381 storming London with pitchforks and righteous fury, we've never liked being told what to do by people in funny clothes.

Fast forward to the 1970s. Enter the Sex Pistols, gobbing into the microphone and swearing on live telly. They didn't just offend the establishment, they gave it a migraine. Johnny Rotten didn't care about your sensibilities. He cared about shaking things up.

Then came Brexit. The modern, bureaucratic version of shouting, "Up yours!" at Brussels while simultaneously trying to remember what WTO rules are.

They still don't understand it. The elites. The chardonnay class. The Davos drones. They thought the people would quietly accept mass censorship, wokery, gender woo, climate doom-mongering and illegal immigration. But we didn't.

Because British rebellion doesn't wear balaclavas. It wears sarcasm. It takes the piss. It dresses up as Winston Churchill for a protest and shouts Shakespearean insults at politicians hiding behind armed guards and lanyards.

We are the land of Orwell and Huxley. Of Roald Dahl and Ricky Gervais. We do freedom of speech with a side of insult and a pint of satire. When comedy dies, tyranny lives. And when free speech lives, tyranny weeps into its soy latte.

Rebellion is waving a flag not because you're nostalgic, but because you're defiant. It's telling the UN to shove their Sustainable Development Goals somewhere very dark and very net-zero. It's rejecting digital ID schemes with a raised eyebrow and a middle finger. It's remembering your nan fought the Luftwaffe with a rolling pin and some leftover dripping.

Cancel culture, Big Pharma, identity politics, thought policing, woke institutions, and DEI dogma, they're all just the latest flavour of tyranny. But they're no match for the British spirit. We are the nation of Churchill's growl, of every unbothered bloke who's ever shouted, "This is bollocks!" from the back of a bus.

So, if you've ever doubted whether you're allowed to say what you think, laugh at what you want, or be who you are, this is your permission slip. It's a declaration. You are British. That means rebellion isn't a choice. It's your bloody birthright.

We didn't fight off Nazis, invent satire, and export rock 'n' roll just to end up apologising for our opinions to some bloke in HR.

So, sharpen your tongue. Polish your backbone. Wave the flag. Not out of nostalgia, but as an act of resistance. Because when the tyrants come with their rules, their fact-checkers, and their digital leash, you say what every glorious Brit before you has said:

"Not today, sunshine."

This is our island. This is our moment. And if they think they can cancel Britain, they are gravely mistaken.

The rebellion is here. And it's bloody magnificent.

And you, my father,
There on the sad height,
Curse, bless, me now
With your fierce tears, I pray.
Do not go gentle
Into that good night.
Rage, rage against
The dying of the light.

— Dylan Thomas

Top Rebellion Tips

1. Start Every Conversation with, "As a Proud Extremist..." and Watch the Soy Lattes Tremble

Forget ,"Hi, how are you?" That's for people who still trust the BBC. From now on, kick off every meeting, dinner party or PTA gathering with, "As a proud extremist who believes women have wombs and taxes are too high..."

It's amazing how quickly the quinoa crowd will pretend to get a phone call from their therapist. You'll clear out your local café quicker than a Brexit vote in Islington. And the beauty of it? You haven't said anything controversial — just common sense, served on a plate of sarcasm with a side of 'deal with it.'

2. Wear a Union Jack Like a Cape and Shop in Aldi Like You're Churchill's Ghost Back for Round Two

Forget subtlety. Wrap yourself in the flag like a rebellious superhero. The type that drinks PG Tips, refuses a smart meter, and rolls their eyes at climate hysteria. March down the frozen aisle like you're storming Berlin, and if anyone gives you a funny look, tell them you're defending the realm from bureaucrats, busybodies, and Brussels sprouts grown under net-zero compliance.

If they still look horrified, start quoting Churchill, "We shall fight them on the bread aisle." If that doesn't shift them, pretend to be confused about your carbon footprint and offer them a bag for life made of beef jerky.

3. Replace Every 'Sorry' in Your Work Emails with 'Sod Off' and Watch HR Weep into Their Wokeness

"Sorry for the delay." No. Try, "Sod off, I was busy defending Western civilisation."

"Sorry if that caused offence." Absolutely not. Try, "If that caused offence, congratulations, you're still alive."

Use your email signature to quote Orwell, Kipling, or your nan. Sign off with: *'Views expressed are entirely my own, and probably yours too if you had the balls to say them out loud.'*

If HR invites you in for a chat, show up with a flask of Yorkshire Tea, a printout of the Magna Carta, and the calm assurance of a Brit who knows their rights and isn't afraid to go full courtroom Boudica if provoked.

4. Live So Loudly, the Thought Police Need Earplugs and a Therapy Llama Just to Read Your File

You want to honour Britain? Don't go quietly. Speak your mind like it's the national anthem. Wear your opinions like medals.

Raise your kids like they're future freedom fighters, not pronoun experiments in a state-run TikTok lab. Laugh in the face of cancellation, mock tyranny with a grin, and when the censors come knocking, greet them with a cup of tea and a list of your unfiltered thoughts, laminated.

Be the reason they panic at Davos. Be the person the 77th Brigade has to assign an extra staff member for. Be so defiantly, brilliantly yourself that even Orwell would stand up and applaud from the afterlife.

Because rebellion isn't just a chapter in our history. It's a birthright, a duty, and the reason we are here in this moment. So go forth, glorious extremist. Raise the roof, raise eyebrows, and most importantly... raise the next generation of lionhearts who'll never ask permission to be free.

Also by Mike Fairclough

The Hero's Voice
Finding the Courage to Speak Out

Take Daily
How Supplements Hijack our Health

Playing with Fire
Embracing Risk and Danger in Schools

Wild Thing
Embracing Childhood Traits in Adulthood
for a Happier, More Carefree Life

Rewilding Childhood
Raising Resilient Children Who Are
Adventurous, Imaginative and Free

Printed in Dunstable, United Kingdom